The Effective CEO 2.0

How to hone your focus, prioritize your time, manage your workload and maximize what you get done in a day

BYRON MORRISON

Byron Morrison's books may be purchased for educational, business, or sales promotional use. For information, please email byron@byronmorrison.com.

First published 2024.

First edition.

Designed and edited by Iulia Protesaru.

ISBN 9798332977343

Contents

A note from the author

This book is a great starting point in helping you master the mental game needed to be a highly effective CEO.

Does this sound like the situation you're in right now?

- You're feeling stretched thin, overloaded and overwhelmed by everything that needs to get done
- You have so many competing priorities that you often get stuck spinning your wheels or doing tasks that don't lead to growth
- You're highly reactive and a lot of your days are spent putting out fires and dealing with other people's problems
- You get times where you overthink, second guess yourself, struggle making decisions and procrastinate, avoiding what you know you need to do
- You're not clearly communicating, setting expectations or keeping people accountable
- You struggle with balance and even when you do take time off you're attached to phone thinking about work

If this sounds like you, then I'd love to take a moment to talk to you about how beyond this book I can help you get this under control.

I developed the Evolved program for CEOs who want to become more effective in their role. Using my battle-tested 5-step Evolved Method, I want to evolve you into the CEO your business needs to break through to the next level of success.

Working directly with me, I'll help you change the way you think, how you process problems, navigate challenges, manage people and perform in your role.

By the end, you'll be able to maximize your time, lead with confidence and grow a business without losing your sanity.

Just a few of the things we'll do include:

- Figure out what you need to prioritize then implement the right processes to effectively delegate, manage your workload, defend your time and maximize what you can get done
- Up-level your leadership skills to improve how you handle tough conversations, communicate expectations, bring out the best in your team and hold people accountable
- Break through the mental blocks that cause you to procrastinate, overthink and doubt yourself, so that you can consistently take the actions you need to take
- Get you out of a reactive state so that you can stop, process problems and calmly respond to them, allowing you to feel more in control with less stress and anxiety
- Develop the right habits and routines to help you feel energized, stay focused, manage stress and feel your best inside and out
- Implement 'Ideal Life Creation' so that you can find balance, switch off, put the right boundaries in place and enjoy the success you worked so hard for

This is how I'm going to help you take control of your life and business, so that you can become the leader your business needs to take it to the next level of success.

The Evolved Method has been implemented by CEOs in 18 different countries by CEOs running everything from tech to SAAS and AI companies, real estate businesses, 7-figure agencies, financial institutions and billion-dollar unicorns in Silicon Valley.

Here's what a few of my clients had to say about the process:

Cole (CEO): *"When something so transformative or someone so transformative enters your life it's really hard to put that impact in words right and that's that's how I felt about this entire experience working with you…As a Founder as a CEO as a person I could not more highly recommend working with Byron because it'll change your life, it's as simple as that. It couldn't be more of an honor or a pleasure to be able to call him a coach, a mentor a friend and a person you won't meet many people if any people in your life who are better human beings than this man is. So thank you Byron for everything that you've done everything you continue to do."*

Ron (CEO): *"After working with Byron and him offering the tools and rewiring my mindset, I have now come back as a more confident leader, I have learned how to defend my schedule, I've learned how to be less reactive, but to also to be able to just pause and look at situations and come up with a better plan, a better solution. I've set new standards…and I'm very confident that Byron is going to change your life for the better".*

Jordan (CEO): *"When I first started working with Byron, I really didn't feel like I was where I wanted to be. I felt like things were out of control, I didn't know how to get my life of working 80 hours and was struggling to spend enough time with my family. I was really trying to get that back, and what I found was that so much of what I didn't feel in control of, I had the ability to get in control of by changing the way I thought about things, by changing the way I approached situations, how present I was, having a true vision for my future, having action plan that really allowed me to recapture that control, to get organised, to come into meetings and be with my family, everything improved."*

Max (Tech CEO): *"Honestly, it's been one of the best decisions I've made. Certainly, compared to the financial investment the value that's come out of it has been astounding."*

Tyler (Business owner): *"I feel like I've left this universe and gone into a different one. It's been incredible…If you judge my level of happiness, clarity, sleep cycle, relationships, confidence, or every other area of my life, it's an easy win. My direction in life has completely changed".*

Rosemary (Business leader): *"I don't feel like I have control back, I feel like I have it for the first time. I used to be fighting all these fires and battles and it was exhausting. As everything felt out of my control and I was miserable. Now I feel calm and like that fire is merely a distraction that I know I can handle."*

Michael (CEO): *"I've gone from completely tired, exhausted, drained to back to my old self so to speak and with more purpose. I'm glad I did it, I certainly know that if I didn't, I'd probably still be in that state of unhappiness and stress. It was the best money I've ever spent on myself".*

Neil (Business owner): *"I now feel completely different, I feel clear-headed and able to focus on the stuff I work out that I should be focusing on, I don't jump around anywhere near as much...I'm in control".*

Lauren (CEO): *"You said you'd make me a better leader and you did. The time we've spent has been invaluable and our sessions are always exactly what I need to calibrate and process problems".*

Josh (Business leader): *"People around me recognised that I'm more effective than I've ever been".*

Are you next?

Joining is by application only, to discuss next steps get in touch at **byron@byronmorrison.com**

Find out more and apply at:
https://www.byronmorrison.com/evolved-program

Before you get started

Before you dive into this book, there are two actions to take that will accelerate your progress and amplify your results.

Action 1: Download the Resources

Included with this book are various bonuses to help you on this journey.

These bonuses have been specifically included to help you take what you learn and implement it at a higher level.

They include "The Effective CEO 2.0 Digital Planner" as well as training videos on "The Effective CEO Planning Process", "The CEO Time Audit Process", "Energy Management Strategies for CEOs" and more.

You can access your bonuses at:

https://byronmorrison.com/ceobonuses

Action 2: Connect on social

I have a YouTube channel and a series called "The Effective CEO". On here you'll find videos covering everything from figuring out what to delegate and prioritize to ways to defend your time, decision-making frameworks, habits of highly effective CEOs, planning your day and so much more.

Watch them now at:
https://www.youtube.com/@ByronMorrison

Every day on social media I share videos, posts and content diving further into what it takes to become a highly effective CEO.

You can also connect with me and follow my content at:

LinkedIn:
https://www.linkedin.com/in/authorbyronmorrison/

Facebook:
https://www.facebook.com/byronmorrisonauthor/

Instagram
https://www.instagram.com/authorbyronmorrison

You can also join the "Impact Driven CEOs" Community, where you can exchange ideas, meet other CEOs and get help with challenges at:

https://www.facebook.com/groups/impactdrivenceos

Preface

Why the 2.0?

In 2021 I wrote a book called *The Effective CEO*.

This book changed my life. It's been read in 19 countries (that I know of), and it's been the catalyst for everything that I'm doing today.

There's just one problem…I don't think it's very good.

Don't get me wrong, the content was solid, but my original plan for that book was to use it as a lead magnet to run paid advertising to, as a way to get consulting clients.

Because of that, the whole project was an experiment and it went from idea to launch in less than five weeks.

Initially, it was also just meant to be about how to figure out what to focus on and the productivity system. But it was a bit too short, so for the final third of the book, I added some tools and strategies to fill space. Again, while these all work and I use them with my clients, it was all just thrown together, to get this project out there.

It's funny how you can't predict what will happen, as I never could have imagined how much it would resonate or how well it would go on to do. It was surreal how many messages I got from people saying how much it helped them in their role. How many application calls I had, where people would hold up the book covered in sticky notes and highlights. How many people told me it was one of the only books they've actually finished.

If you're a high achiever you've no doubt been in situations where you've done something and you know that if you'd given it more time it could be so much better. This is in part because of the standards you set for yourself and what you know you're capable of.

That's why when I say "I don't think it's very good" I'm probably being harsh on myself. But it's because I know it wasn't even close to what it could have been.

That book opened up so many opportunities for me, including enabling me to reach a new audience that allowed me to work with CEOs in 17 different countries. Through that experience, I've developed new strategies and frameworks, revised old ones and improved many of the approaches I use. I've also spent thousands more hours coaching and working with CEOs behind closed doors, which gave me a new level of expertise and understanding about what it takes to get someone to perform at their best.

Over the last couple of years, I've wondered what would happen if I redid that book properly. So, I decided to find out. Hence, the 2.0.

If you've read the first version, what you're going to dive into is a completely rewritten book. Some of the content on figuring out what to focus on is similar, but you'll find a completely revamped planning system that will empower you to feel even more in control of your days.

Beyond that, there's a wealth of new concepts, ideas and guidance to help you become more effective in your role. This includes an entire section on effective delegation, communicating expectations and keeping people accountable. The latter part of the book is also focused on what gets in the way of people following through. You'll discover strategies to deal with procrastination and overwhelm, how to set boundaries, structure meetings, defend your time, stop people-pleasing and so much more.

I've taken everything I've discovered over the last few years about the productivity and time management side of helping CEOs become more effective in their role and broken it down in this book for you. So, whether you are a returning reader or picking up my work for the first time, I'm excited to have you here and I hope you enjoy the 2.0 version of *The Effective CEO*.

Introduction

Here's a secret most CEOs don't realize…growth can actually be a huge trap.

A founder or CEO of a small company will generally have more control than a CEO of a scale-up or larger, established business. This doesn't have to be the case, but it often is. The reason is simple - the new levels of problems that come with their growth and success, usually brought on by a growing team, stakeholders to keep happy, more operations and moving parts. That's before you add in all the fires, people constantly coming to you to solve their problems and never-ending daily demands.

When you're going through this period of growth, you tend to take on more responsibilities. You work longer hours. Put more pressure on yourself. Push yourself harder. And sure, business will continue to grow. But you'll end up dreading any time the phone rings. You'll resent your team every time they ask for help on a problem they should know how to handle. Worst of all, you'll stop enjoying your business, as it'll feel like a never-ending mental and emotional drain. Yet you'll keep telling yourself that once you reach the next level, it'll be easier. That then, you'll let go, you'll have more time, you'll feel more in control. I call this the *overwhelmed CEO trap*, as that next level just brings more challenges, problems and demands, causing you to get stuck in a repeating cycle where you feel like you're behind again, and again.

Do you know what the biggest bottleneck is in most businesses?

I'll give you a clue, it's not the wrong strategy, poor market conditions or even difficulties hiring the right people. Instead, the biggest bottleneck in most businesses is…the CEO. Because when they're not performing at the level they need to, that's when decisions get stalled, opportunities get lost, frustrations build within the team and internally, the business starts to crack and fall apart.

I discovered this the hard way. After my dad's cancer took me on a journey of transformation, I wrote my first best-selling book and started a company focused on helping people from around the world to live healthier and happier lives. While I was great at the helping people part, truth be told, I was completely in over my head when it came to running a business. I'd never made big decisions or dealt with such high levels of pressure. I'd never navigated problems that had huge repercussions, dealt with such a large workload or had so many people I had to deliver for. Nothing I'd done before had prepared me for the deep end I jumped into, and it felt like I was essentially winging it.

I started that business with a desire to change and impact the world, yet instead my days became all about solving other people's problems and dealing with never-ending demands. It was exhausting, and I remember days where I'd look at my calendar with a feeling of dread over whatever fire I needed to face next.

Before long, I found myself burnt out and going through the motions, where every single day was a battle that *I just needed to get through*. Instead of slowing down though, my solution was to just keep pushing. After all, I had so much to get done, that I was convinced I couldn't stop. I kept telling myself "If I can just get this right, then everything will fall into place." It never did.

Eventually, I reached a point where I started to question if any of it was really worth it. This feeling was amplified by my complete lack of work-life balance.

With so much to do, I was working 60+ hour weeks, but even when I did take time off, I'd be attached to my phone and thinking about work. I remember going to a wedding and spending half the time on my phone responding to messages. Going on holiday and waking up early to cram in a few hours of work. Missing out on events with friends as I had to work late. Even in the times I was there physically, mentally I was consumed by the thought of what needed to get done. This was nowhere close to the life of freedom I'd imagined when I started. Looking back, it's no wonder that my business felt like a mental and emotional drain.

All of this led to huge problems in every area of my life. My relationships were disconnected, my energy was completely drained, I wasn't looking after myself and I'd stopped enjoying what I was doing. I didn't want to throw in the towel, but I also knew I couldn't carry on this way. I looked at some of the greatest business leaders and saw that many of them were confident, composed and, from the outside, they looked like they had it all together. I was determined to figure out what they did to get this under control. To do so, I became a student of everything from leadership to managing people, mindset, high performance and emotional resilience. I read books, did courses, got coached and mentored, all to figure out how to become the leader my business needed.

What this deep work ultimately revealed to me was that the problem, was me. Even though I was ridiculously *busy*, I was so stuck in the weeds that I was spinning my wheels and not actually moving anything of value forward. To make matters worse, I'd often get stuck in my own head too, overthinking decisions, second-guessing myself and avoiding the actions I knew I needed to take. As a result, growth would stall, decisions would get postponed and I'd lose hours every day not doing the things I knew I needed to do. I'm sure you've had days like that yourself, where just being in that mental state is exhausting and it feels more tiring than a day digging ditches.

One of my favorite quotes is "Your business growth will never outgrow your inner growth". It was only when I learned how to evolve myself, that I was able to get the challenges that came with my role under control. By doing so, I managed to grow and scale my company, all while taking back control of the other areas of my life. I was able to reconnect with those around me, reignite my passion for what I was doing and finally start enjoying the success I worked so hard for.

At the time I was working with a lot of entrepreneurs, CEOs and business leaders on their health and wellbeing. Naturally, as we dived into the reasons why they were burnt out, struggling to sleep, stressed and drained of energy, the challenges they faced in their role started to surface. I found that helping them navigate them was not only my superpower, it was also what I loved to do. This is why the natural evolution of my work has been to help CEOs navigate the challenges that come with their growth. At the time of writing, I've been fortunate to work with leaders in 17 countries, ranging from founders to tech CEOs, CEOs running global production companies, SAAS and AI companies, financial institutions, 7-figure agencies, real estate businesses and billion-dollar unicorns in Silicon Valley. What this has allowed me to do is gain unique insights and experience dealing with problems discussed behind closed doors that very few people in the world will even be aware of, let alone have been exposed to.

That's why I decided to write this book, to pass on to you what I've learned about becoming a more effective CEO. Now, you may be thinking "Byron if you've never grown a billion-dollar company how can you advise me on how to navigate my role?" It's a valid question and it's why from the get-go I want to be clear – I am not a business coach. It's not my job to tell a CEO how to run or grow their company. After all, they're the CEO for a reason. What I am an expert in is people, productivity, communication and high performance. This is key, because what most people don't realize is that so many of the day-to-day problems CEOs face are around managing their team, conflicts, defending their time and getting others to follow through.

This is why CEOs hire me when they want to become the leader their business needs to take it to the next level of success. In this work, we don't talk about strategies, their product or what they're doing with the business. Instead, it's my job to put the focus on them and how they show up in everything they do. It's like if you had a problem with your foot, you wouldn't go to another CEO for guidance. Instead, you'd go to *a specialist who has dedicated themselves to knowing how to fix the problem*. Much like how elite athletes have coaches who themselves haven't played in the major leagues, CEOs and leaders also benefit of the guidance of those who have spent their lives figuring out what it takes to become the best at it. This is why I've been fortunate to work with clients across such a broad range of industries, as the work they do is actually irrelevant. Instead, our focus is on them and how they execute on what needs to get done.

I share this upfront because I want to set the right expectations. Because if you're looking for a book on scaling strategies or growth hacks, you're in the wrong place. This book is all about productivity, helping you get more out of your days and ensuring that you can perform at the level needed to be a highly effective CEO.

I find that the average client who applies what I am going to share with you takes back control of five to 15 hours a week. The side effect being that it then frees them up to create more growth, generate more revenue and make more impact, all with less stress and overwhelm. So in many ways, *amplifying your effectiveness may very well be the growth hack you've been missing all along.*

With that being said, you being here shows that you recognize that your current way of operating isn't working. At least not as effectively as you'd like. Because of that, this book is going to challenge you to think differently and change how you approach problems. One thing my private clients love about my approach is that it's not just theoretical, it's incredibly practical. My aim of this book is to replicate that philosophy, so instead of just giving you motivational fluff, I want to ensure that you can apply what I share with you.

To help you do that, in this book you'll find actionable exercises and tasks that will take you step-by-step through everything I'm sharing with you. If you want to get the most out of this book, then I highly encourage you to commit to following through with them, as it's in the doing that you'll create the clarity and transformation that will enable you to regain control. I'll also go through real-world examples and case studies of clients who have implemented these strategies, along with how I guided them, and what they needed to think about to get their situation under control. The purpose of this is to get you to see the changes in action, as that will give you a better idea about how to approach these concepts yourself. Obviously, due to confidentiality reasons, names will be altered and any details that could link the client to a specific company will be left out.

Now, this book is primarily geared towards CEOs and leaders in the first few years of their positions. However, whether you are a seasoned executive or even someone aspiring to advance in your career, you will still find concepts and ideas that you can implement to become more effective in your role.

What you're going to discover

This book will be divided into six different sections.

Section 1 will help you figure out what you need to focus on and prioritize so that you can be clear on where you need to spend your days and what you need to let go of.

Section 2 will dive into effective delegation, clear communication and keeping people accountable.

Section 3 is about energy management and strategies to consistently perform at your best, without burning out.

Section 4 will go through the Effective CEO Planning Process and how to structure your days, weeks and months to maximize what you get done.

Section 5 will focus on mindset strategies to ensure you follow through. These will range from ways to deal with procrastination and overwhelm to setting boundaries, defending your time and running effective meetings.

Section 6 will pull it all together and show you how you need to evolve as a leader to break through to the next level of success.

Additional help and support

If along the way you have any questions, or if you want to find out how I may be able to help you directly, then drop me an email at **byron@byronmorrison.com** and I'll personally get back to you.

Also, if you're a first-time CEO feeling stretched thin, overwhelmed or like you're not performing at the level you know you could (or need to) then my Evolved program may be for you. Working directly with me, I'm going to help you become the leader your business needs, so that you can maximize your time, lead with confidence and grow a business without losing your sanity.

If you want to take control and become more effective in your role, then you can find out more and apply for a place at:

https://www.byronmorrison.com/evolved-program

Now that we've got all that covered, let's begin.

Section 1

Honing your focus

The truth about your "time" problem

Every week I speak to CEOs who tell me they never have enough minutes in the day to get everything done. Because of it, they want help implementing the right systems to manage their time and strategies to be more productive. I get it, when you're running a company it can feel like you have so much on your plate that you're running backward on a treadmill trying to catch up. That's probably why you decided to buy this book, so that you too can take control of your days. Now, don't worry, because reclaiming your time and helping you get more done is going to be a huge focus of what we cover. What I've found from speaking to and working with so many people, is that in this situation, you tend to either convince yourself that something is the problem, or you overlook the root cause and contributing factors that are amplifying the issue. That's why as your coach and guide in this journey, it's going to be my job at times to challenge your way of thinking or shift your perspective. With that in mind, I want you to take a moment to consider…

What if time (or lack thereof), isn't actually the problem?

What if instead, there is a different issue that's *causing* the lack of time?

I'll give you a real-world example to help you answer these questions. Jamie reached out to me when his business was going through an explosive period of growth. He was a founder who had developed a product, taken it to market, secured several big raises and now they were scaling. Now, on top of driving growth, he also had to manage a team, keep stakeholders happy and overlook the day-to-day operations, all while dealing with what felt like a million different fires each day. To try and get everything done, he was working 60+ hour weeks, yet regardless of how much time he put in, he could never catch up.

Jamie had never been a CEO before, so with so many unknowns and new challenges, he hired me because he wanted support in becoming more productive. When we dove into it, I uncovered that he was in the overwhelmed CEO trap, stretching himself thin and overloading himself. With so much to do, he'd try to attack the day with no real plan or intention for what he should be doing. As a result, he was highly reactive, allowing life and tasks to happen to him, where he'd often drop what he needed to do to put out fires or solve other people's problems.

To make matters worse, when he wasn't firefighting, he'd spend his days bouncing around from one task to the next. One minute he'd be working on a report, then he'd be responding to emails, then he'd be pulled into a meeting. It felt like his brain had hundreds of tabs open, all with competing thoughts, ideas and priorities. On top of that, the stress he was under was amplified by their business' newfound growth. The higher stakes were causing him to second-guess himself at every turn and overthink key decisions, making the paralyzing effect even worse. Before long, the pressure and anxiety that came with the day would cause him to mentally shut down. So instead of doing what he needed to get done, he'd allow himself to get consumed by busywork, procrastinate watching YouTube, or mindlessly scroll through the newsfeed. While he did feel constantly busy, when we broke it down, it became clear that he wasn't actually getting much done. Not much of value anyway.

There is a HUGE difference between being busy and being productive. So many people confuse the two as they find comfort in ticking things off and getting stuff done, even if they're not really moving anything forward. Like so many other overwhelmed CEOs, I completely understood why Jamie thought he had a time problem. In reality though, he had an *effectiveness* problem, as he wasn't making the best use of the time he had. That's why even though he was working 60+ hour weeks, he was only getting about 15 hours of productive, high-value work done. The rest? He was doing busywork: stop-starting tasks, trying to make other people happy or losing time stuck in his head. This is something I see all the time in the CEOs who come to me for help, where most of their days are filled with tasks or actions that aren't driving the business forward.

You may be in a similar situation yourself, where despite being constantly busy, you look back on your days and weeks and you don't know what you did with them. That's why before we go any further, I want you to take a moment to be brutally honest with yourself.

Thinking back over what you did over the last seven days, how many of those hours truly mattered? As in, the time you spent produced high-value work that grew your business, impacted your bottom line, or furthered your vision?

How many of those hours were spent on tasks that didn't lead to growth or on solving problems you shouldn't have even been involved in?

How much time did you lose to procrastination, lack of focus or simply avoiding what you knew you needed to do?

If you're truly honest with yourself...How *effective* have you truly been over the last few weeks?

I know that recognizing this can be a tough pill to swallow, especially when you face the realization that maybe you aren't as busy or productive as you think you are. I want to be clear though, I don't want you to dwell on the past or beat yourself up over this. After all, what's done is done and there's no point wasting energy worrying about what you can't change. Instead, this is all about holding a mirror up to yourself to get you to realize your situation. After all, often the start of making a change is recognizing what is causing the problem in the first place. Not only that, but you reading this right now is also the first step in turning this around. If anything, it's already a sign that you are actively taking control of the one thing you can. Yourself.

Now, there are a variety of reasons why someone might not be as effective as they could be. These can range from missing certain skills to a fear of letting go, not spending their time on what matters or various other factors in between. I find that often this pattern of overloading themselves happens because someone hasn't fully transitioned to their role or adapted to the changes and responsibilities that come with it. For instance, there's a huge difference between being a founder or manager and being a CEO. When you're a founder or manager, you can get away with doing everything yourself. If anything, you need to if you want to build momentum and grow. What so many first-time CEOs overlook is that as you scale, your focus has to become far more honed in. The reason being is between adding on a growing team, stakeholders and customers, there are so many more responsibilities that come with your growth. When you stack all this on top, there simply aren't enough minutes in the day to do everything.

That's what was happening with Jamie. He was still thinking like a founder, where he was so used to delivering everything himself, that his default mindset was to hustle and grind to get things done. While that worked when he was in the start-up phase, now that they'd scaled, these behaviors were why he was burning himself out and bottlenecking growth.

The thing is, he knew he should delegate more. He knew he should let go. He knew he should get out of the weeds. But no one had taught him how and whenever he tried, people would make mistakes, drop the ball, or not follow through. This is, in part, why he convinced himself it was easier to just do it himself. The good news is that the cause of why he was struggling in his role was totally fixable. He was just missing several key skills, frameworks and mental shifts that would allow him to get out of the trenches. All of which I'll be taking you through in this book.

Part of the reason why Jamie struggled with handing off tasks was that he didn't really know what he should be taking on. In our second session, he asked me "What should I be doing as a CEO?" This is one of the most common questions I get from the CEOs I work with. That's why before we go anything further, we need to figure out where you should be spending your time in the first place, as the insights you gain from that will directly determine everything else we implement that is personal to your situation.

What should you be doing as CEO?

In my experience the answer is...It depends. Yes, you need to set the vision, drive the strategy, bring together the right team and make sure everything is functioning. But beyond that, every CEO is different, with varying skills, strengths and weaknesses. Many of the CEOs I work with struggle with prioritization because they haven't clearly defined their role and responsibilities. Because of it, they just take on tasks without stopping to think whether they should, need to, or if they're a good use of time.

At the end of the day, you are either going to do a few things really well, or many things mediocre or badly. That's why we have to get you clear on what you need to focus on to drive the business forward.

To do this, there are three things you need to clarify:

1) What is your zone of genius?
2) Where does your time have the greatest impact?
3) What can only be done by you?

What is your zone of genius?

If you think about your journey and what got you to where you are today, what has been your unfair advantage or unique set of skills that has massively contributed to your growth? Think about it. What is your superpower? What is it that you do best, that when you operate in that area you see amazing traction and results? That is your zone of genius.

For every CEO this is going to be different, as for one it may be sales and business development, whereas for another it could be marketing or product development. So, knowing yourself, what do you excel at? Figuring this out is essential, as this will be a key indicator of where you need to be prioritizing your time.

To help you think about this on a deeper level, I'll give you a real-world example. When Stephen and I had this conversation, it was clear that he was incredible at business development. He was amazing at connecting with people, converting new customers and driving revenue. Yet when we looked at his day-to-day, he was spending most of his time on administrative tasks, trying to solve other people's problems or attending meetings he really didn't need to be present for.

Yes, all these tasks were important, but he had an amazing team around him who he simply wasn't utilizing. With goals of doubling in size over the next 12 months, it was clear he needed to be client-facing and driving revenue, not involved in everyday tasks that could be done by someone else. Not letting go or delegating meant that he was operating outside of his zone of genius, which in turn was negatively impacting their bottom line and growth. It was also causing frustrations in the team, as he was stepping on their toes and allowing his over-involvement to get in the way of what they needed to deliver. By recognizing what his zone of genius was, we were then able to sit down and create a plan to get nearly everything else off his plate. A shift that over the next 12 months allowed them to increase their turnover by 130%, all while removing a huge amount of pressure and stress that Stephen was placing on himself.

As for what your zone of genius is, the answer may not be immediately clear for everyone. You may need some time to think about it. If need be, go for a walk, allow yourself to journal, meditate, perhaps speak to your team or a mentor. Do whatever you need to do to figure this out.

Where does your time have the greatest impact?

Ask yourself "Where does my time have the greatest impact?" As in, if you spent more of your days doing this particular thing, it would massively impact your growth, revenue or stability. With my clients, I've seen this range from devising the strategy to spending time with their team to ensure they have the support they need. It could also include marketing, liaising with investors or building relationships with potential customers. Chances are that your greatest impact will overlap with your zone of genius. That may not always be the case though, which is why it helps to think about this separately. That way you can ensure you don't overlook anything of value that you should be doing in your role.

What can only be done by you?

There will be tasks in the company that fall outside of your superpowers, yet given the leadership position you are in, you still need to do them. These could be anything from strategic decisions to running board meetings or other obligations which you *have to do*.

To figure this out, it helps to look at your recurring tasks and to reflect on the past few weeks. That way you can create a list of everything that was mission-critical and that could not have been done by someone else.

Task before moving forward

Defining your role and knowing where you should be spending your time is essential, as we'll be using that clarity to determine what to delegate, let go of and how to manage your workload to maximize your time. You can also use these insights for future hires, as you may want the next iterations of your team to be built around people who excel in areas you are weak in, or who can take over tasks that either you shouldn't or don't want to do.

Before you go any further, make sure you are clear on:
1) What is your zone of genius?
2) Where does your time have the greatest impact?
3) What can only be done by you?

Auditing your time

Now that you know what you *should* be doing, it's time to figure out what you are *actually* doing. Because when it comes to being an effective CEO, what you don't do, is just as important as what you do. In fact, this is so important that I'll say it again in bold:

When it comes to being an effective CEO, what you don't do, is just as important as what you do.

So many CEOs I speak to are so stuck in the day-to-day that they don't even recognize how much their actions and decisions are impacting their business's growth and long-term success. I've found that this isn't just because they're trying to do too much, but also because of the need to keep up a perception of how hard they are working. Many of the CEOs I help have the belief they need to be the first one in and last one out, just to show others that they too are putting in the work. This goes back to that hustler mentality of trying to get things done, where you convince yourself that if you want to be successful, then you have to put in the time.

While your intentions may be in the right place, the reality is that *hard work is not the secret to success*. After all, how many hard-working people do you know who are broke or living paycheck to paycheck? If hard work was all it took, then wouldn't they all be rich and wildly successful?

Don't get me wrong, of course working hard is important, but ultimately, it's what you do with your time that truly matters. This is why working crazy hours just for the sake of it is not a great idea. Firstly, if you want to be a highly effective CEO, then your time should not be spent on busywork or being stuck in the trenches. Instead, it should be on the high-value tasks that drive the business forward. Secondly, after a while, your focus has diminishing returns, so something that could take 20 minutes, can end up taking several hours. Not only is this taking time away from the tasks that truly matter, but it will often leave you lacking the energy or bandwidth to execute on what will actually move the needle.

Obviously, I'm not saying don't work hard. Because there's no way around it, if you want to create a business that changes the world, it is going to take a huge amount of time and effort to make it happen. At the end of the day though, your value as a CEO doesn't just come from the hours you put in. Instead, it comes from the ideas you bring, the people you inspire and the impact you create. Doing that results from being highly intentional with your time and ensuring your focus is in the right place. This is why this time audit is so important, as it'll give you a better understanding of what you've been doing and what you need to change to take control for the future.

When I'm helping CEOs figure this out, I tend to use the example of Matthew, who had a huge breakthrough in our initial conversation. During our call, he told me about how one of the biggest challenges he's facing is that now his team is growing, he's getting sucked into solving lower-level problems and handholding. The reason why this is causing frustration is that both the amount of money he earns personally and the business's bottom line are directly tied to the time he spends with clients. Meaning whenever his focus is on something else, both him and the business are losing money.

I asked him, "How much time is this taking up each day?" He responded, "About an hour." So I asked him, "How much is that costing you?" He paused for a moment, then said "That's a great question. I've never thought of it like that." He grabbed his calculator and did some math. By dividing his income by the average number of hours he works and multiplying it by fifty-two weeks, he figured out that his time is worth $1,500 an hour. Meaning those distractions are personally costing him $1,500 a day! That's $7,500 a week! And $390,000 a year! That's a huge impact on not just how much he earns personally, but also the business's revenue. It's not just a one-off either. If left unresolved, it will compound, and as the business and team continue to grow, these tasks will likely take up even more of his day. If he was more defensive with his time and was able to reduce those five hours per week down to say two, then he could increase his income by an extra $234,000 a year. Before we spoke, he didn't even realize the true extent of his problem and it was merely just a frustration he had been accepting.

Now, your income may not be like Matthew's, where it is directly linked to the time you spend with clients. Regardless, focusing on the wrong things will no doubt be costing you and the business revenue and growth. I had a client who before our conversation, didn't even register that over 70% of her time was being spent on trying to solve other people's problems. 70%! That meant that the bulk of her time that should have been spent on strategy, raising funds or leading the business, was instead being spent on handling management issues and dealing with fires.

This is why you need to sit down and figure out what you've actually been doing and where you've been spending your days. Chances are you're spending more time than you realize on things that you shouldn't.

How to audit your time

The way I approach this with private clients is by looking at how they spend their time from two angles: the past and the future. This way, we figure out what they have been doing that needs to stop, as well as what they are planning to do that must come off their plate immediately.

I have a training video called *The CEO Time Audit Process* which will take you step-by-step through everything I'm about to share with you. It's included as one of the free bonuses that come with this book, so if you'd like to revisit this process in video format, you can get it at:

https://byronmorrison.com/ceobonuses

Auditing the past

What you need to do is reflect on exactly what you did over the past three to four weeks. Look back on your calendar, emails and diary to get clear on everything you did, from what meetings you were in, to the tasks you took on, events you attended and everything else you did to fill your days. You can either go through them one at a time or create a list. Then looking at them through the lens of your zone of genius, where your time has the greatest impact and what can only be done by you, ask yourself:

1) Was this a good use of your time? As in, did getting this done have a positive impact on the business, drive revenue or further your targets?

Next think about:

2) Did this need to be done by you, did you need to be involved, or could this have been done by someone else?

Part of the problem with being so busy is that it's easy to get into the cycle where you have tasks or activities that you just do on autopilot without really thinking about why you're doing them. I often find with clients that when we audit their time, they realize that there are meetings they don't need to be in, projects they shouldn't be working on, or just day-to-day tasks they need to hand off. There may also be things you are doing that were part of your previous responsibilities or that your business needed you to do a few years ago, yet now they aren't worth your or your team's time. That's why if you don't stop to look at what you are doing, then you risk continuing to be engaged in activities that are having a negative ROI on your time.

I'll give you a few examples of CEOs who had massive realizations from this, which helped them reclaim several hours every single week.

When Frank first started his company, the way he got customers and grew the business was through going to networking events. This is how he met people, built connections and spread the word about what they were doing. Over the last few years though, the business had pivoted and they'd automated the majority of their marketing through paid advertising and other methods. Also, their new products and offerings were targeting a different market, making networking events ineffective in reaching those customers. Frank was so used to attending these events that he never stopped to ask himself whether or not he should. For him, not only were these events having a negative ROI on his time (since that time could be used for higher-value tasks), they were also mentally draining and something he dreaded waking up to do. Upon realizing this, he felt a huge weight lifted in the relief that he could stop attending them altogether.

Martin's background was in sales, and as part of scaling his company, twelve months prior he had onboarded a new sales team. As this was his zone of genius, he was heavily involved in training them to ensure they could perform and deliver. A big part of this meant he was spending many hours a week in sales meetings and listening to calls. He was also being CC'd extensively in customer-facing email chains to monitor and give feedback to the team on their approach. It was a lot to do and simply keeping on top of it all was exhausting. A few months ago, all of this was no doubt important, but he realized that the team were crushing their targets and it was time to take off the training wheels. What that meant was that Martin could remove himself from the majority of these meetings and communicate to the team that they no longer needed to include him in email chains. Instead, if they had any issues, they could reach out to him directly. This simple shift alone got him back over eight hours a week. Upon our conversations, it dawned on him that if he had thought about this sooner, he could have reduced his involvement several months ago. Getting out of these activities was just the start of Martin taking back control of his time. By the end of our 90 days working together he had reclaimed over 15 hours a week. That essentially allows him to get an extra week and a half worth of work done every month. He's not alone either, as I find that the average client I work with regains 5 to 15 hours a week. That's time they can use to drive more revenue, create more impact and live a life of freedom on their terms.

This is why it's so important that you get clear on both what you need to do, as well as what you need to stop doing. People create a to-do list all the time for the things they need to get done. What they don't factor in are the tasks they're doing which are not a good use of their days. This is why I love the idea of creating a *Not-to-do list* of all the things you are committing to no longer doing.

It's important to note this isn't just applicable to your business. Instead, there may be tasks you are doing in your personal life that simply aren't a good use of your time or that are getting in the way of other things you could or want to do. For instance, let's say you are training for a fitness event, while also balancing running a company and being a parent. Inevitably, there will be areas of your like that will have to give. In this case, let's say you'd struggle with your diet, as it is consuming a lot of time trying to prepare healthy meals that fuel your intense training schedule. A temporary solution could be to sign up to a meal delivery service to handle this part of your life and take the pressure off. This would then give you that time back so that you can use it to focus on running the business, training and spending time with your family. Therefore, bulk cooking and meal planning need to be on your *Not-to-do list* until the fitness event finishes.

Task before moving forward

Audit the last three to four weeks, looking at everything from regular meetings to events, tasks you did and where you spent your days, then ask yourself: Is this something you needed to be involved in? Was this a good use of your time? Could this have been done by someone else?

With some items, it may be easy to remove yourself straight away, like a regular meeting you don't need to be in. With others, you may need to have conversations to delegate these tasks and create accountability processes to ensure people follow through with them. We'll be getting to how to do all of that shortly. For now, figure out your *Not to-do list* and what would need to happen for you to get out of these tasks.

It's important to note that as your business and team grow, your role and responsibilities will grow with them. That's also why it's essential that you take a few minutes each week or at least commit to taking some time once a month to reflect on what you did and how you've been spending your time.

Auditing the future

Now that you've audited the past, it's time to shift your focus to the present and the future to get clear on where you're about to spend your time. To audit the future, we are going to split this into two separate actions: examine your upcoming week and gain clarity on your *real* to-do list.

First, look ahead at your diary and calendar to see anything you have committed to in the next seven days that is out of alignment with your goals or not a good use of your time. Depending on the insights you gained from auditing the past, there may be meetings or events you determined you should no longer be a part of. I had this conversation with a client recently who realized that the weekly marketing meeting was not something he needed to be part of. Instead, his team could make decisions and then email him a summary. Historically he'd been on the attendee list, so the meeting was recurring weekly in his calendar by default. By auditing the week ahead he was able to delete it, freeing up the slot for use when he came to planning his week.

When doing this, you may also see other items that shouldn't be part of your schedule. I saw this in a recent conversation with Darren, where upon looking ahead, he saw he had a lunch meeting with a new contact. Someone he knew had asked him for a favor to meet with this individual, to see if there were ways they could potentially do business together. One of the biggest challenges Darren and I were working on was his people pleasing tendencies. Because of it, he'd say yes far too much to things he knew he shouldn't, then he'd try to cram them in or drop what he needed to do. This meeting was a prime example of that and with a stacked week ahead, he was already resenting having to go to it. Upon further discussion, he also realized he wasn't even the best person to meet with this individual, as even if there were opportunities to do business together, his sales team would be better at determining what that could look like. Knowing all this, it was easy to give himself permission to cancel the lunch and instead, he connected him with his sales team to explore further opportunities. The two minutes he spent looking ahead and auditing his future saved him over two hours of having to drive somewhere, park, meet and eat with someone simply as a favor. Not to mention the added stress he would have had from rushing that day to get everything else done.

With so many of the CEOs I work with, I find that their tendency to say yes too much is a big part of the reason why they get stuck in the weeds or involved in tasks that shouldn't be a priority. That's why before you start your week it's vital to look ahead and determine what is not going to be a good use of your time. It's also important to do this now, as leaving it too late risks you just attending out of obligation or being the person who cancels at the last minute, messing other people around.

The next action is to audit everything you need to get done. The way I do this with my private clients is I get them to create a to-do list of everything that's currently on their plate. Then, we go through it point-by-point, looking at whether it's actually something they need to do (is it just busywork?), if it should be delegated (can someone else do it?) or simply removed (does it have to be done in the first place?).

When I got Adam to do this, he came back to me with a list of 46 items. It's no wonder he felt overwhelmed. One of the reasons he had hired me was that he felt completely stretched thin by everything he needed to get done. He'd started the company with a small team of four and over the last 18 months, they'd scaled to over 150 people. Despite that rapid growth, Adam hadn't adapted to his role and he was still stuck in the founder mentality of being involved in everything. This was highly frustrating for his team and there was a running joke in the office that if they asked him for something or to make a decision, it would be at least two weeks before it was done. Not only was he holding up projects, but taking on too much meant he was also dropping the ball on important things as he just couldn't get around to everything. With 46 items on his to-do list for the week, it was no surprise this was happening.

As we worked through the list, it became clear he was involved in too many tasks that were simply not a good use of his time. Like an upcoming event that they were hosting where he needed to reach out to a few people and invite them. Yes, doing this was important, but it's exactly why he had an assistant. With tasks like this, they may only take a few minutes, but having them on his plate was causing him to feel completely overwhelmed by the sheer volume of what he needed to get done. This is why we had to make him far more intentional with what he took on.

To do so, I took him through his to-do list one point at a time, and we answered these questions:

1. Is this actually important? As in, will getting it done have a positive ROI, drive growth or impact the business? If no, remove it.
2. Is this a priority right now? Does it align with your 90-day goals and targets and do you have the energy and bandwidth to commit to this? If no, remove it from your list and set it aside for a later date.
3. If yes, does it need to be done by you?
4. If no, who could or should take over?

In the end, he reduced that 46-item list down to 22. Meaning the 15 minutes we spent on this audit cut his to-do list down by over 50%. Yes, there was still way too much on it and going forward we had to work on his delegation and letting go skills, but as a start, he at least felt like he could breathe, as what was left was far more manageable. Adam is no doubt an extreme example here, but it's not uncommon for other clients to also reduce their to-do lists by half.

This is why before you even think about planning your week, the first task needs to be to complete the future audit and remove calendar time wasters and evaluate your to-do list. This is how you are going to free up time for the tasks that are actually in line with your goals.

I saw this come up as a challenge for Lauren who I'd worked with a few years ago. Her company was approaching its next fundraising round, so she'd rehired me, as she knew that her ability to utilize her time during this period would make or break their success. When we mapped out her goals, she essentially had ten weeks to get everything in order before she needed to start talking to investors and arranging meetings. Lauren was the classic overwhelmed CEO who would overload herself by overcommitting and taking on far too much. This is why we broke down those ten weeks into smaller cycles. This allowed Lauren to get good visibility of her deadlines, in addition to helping her deliver efficiently and keeping her in control. For the first six weeks, she needed to be heavily involved in product development to ensure it was up to the standard needed to showcase it in their pitches. Knowing that, all sales and marketing needed to take a backseat until week seven when they were clear on what they were taking to market. This reduced a lot of the pressure, as prior to this conversation she was trying to figure out how she was going to work on everything at once.

Another thing stressing Lauren was that she had received several emails from past connections and investors asking for an updated pitch deck, as they knew they were about to start fundraising. She told me that she needed to spend some time that week to put it together, as she didn't want to leave them waiting. I had to challenge her thinking here, as the product wasn't complete and she had previously said they weren't ready to share this yet with anyone outside of the organization. The reason she was acting on this was because she was just trying to get tasks off her list. What she should have done first though was slow down and process what she was committing to before taking it on. Upon doing so, she realized that a better decision would be to email the investors saying the pitch deck would be sent out in eight weeks. This gave them enough time to get the product and marketing in place. It also set a deadline for her and the team, as well as a clear expectation for her investors. In addition to this situation, Lauren was feeling pressure from several product demonstration meetings scheduled in her calendar over the coming weeks. Since the product was still being finalized, she didn't feel confident to show it yet to prospects. These meetings had been booked a few weeks prior, so she didn't want to let people down. I once again had to challenge her. Showing an unfinished product would risk losing potential interest and running into quality-related issues since the product hadn't reached the testing phase yet. She agreed, and simply contacted them to reschedule for eight weeks' time. This took a huge amount of pressure off her, all while taking more items off her plate.

Lauren had been operating in a scarcity mindset committing to things just because they felt important or were simply in her calendar. By mapping out her targets for that sprint, defining her timelines and what she needed to take on, it became far easier for her to push back, know what she should commit to and defend her time.

That's why this audit will become one of the most important parts of your week, as the clarity you gain will massively impact your focus and will determine where you spend your time. You can also use this framework throughout the day whenever something new lands on your desk or to check that what you are focusing on is truly a good use of your time, energy and bandwidth. Someone who mastered this way of operating was Corey. When he and I met he was in the classic founder mentality of hustling trying to get stuff done. So when something new landed on his plate, his first thought was that he needed to add it to his to-do list and get it done. By clearly defining everything I've shared with you so far and working on his mindset and delegation skills, now when he gets something new his first thought is "Who else could do it?" A shift that has now made him a self-proclaimed "Delegation Machine".

This change in thinking comes from knowing your zone of genius, being clear on your priorities and then feeling confident that you have the right team and processes in place to get people to follow through. You also need to know your goals and targets, because if you don't, then like Lauren, you risk getting distracted by shiny objects or pulled into things you shouldn't be spending your energy on.

Avoiding shiny objects

When you're running a business chances are that every week you'll be presented with new ideas, opportunities or things you could pursue. With limited time and focus, there are only so many things you can take on. This is where so many people become their own worst enemies, as they allow themselves to become distracted and bounce around between ideas, never fully committing or following through with what they need to do.

The reality is that you are either going to be able to do a few things really well, or many things mediocre or badly. That's why if you want to be highly effective, then what you don't do, is just as important as what you do.

I saw this happening on a coaching call with Stuart. After months of development and hard work, they were only a few weeks away from launching their new product. Yet in one of our sessions, Stuart came to the call excited about a new business opportunity he'd been presented with earlier that week. On paper, the idea sounded fantastic, with great potential. But there was a problem. Getting involved in this was time-sensitive and being this close to launch, he already had enough on his plate. Meaning that taking on more could risk everything they'd been working towards. That's why even though this new idea sounded great, with limited capacity and bandwidth, he needed to say no and defend his time. By doing so he was able to ensure his focus was where it needed to be to have a successful launch.

In my first session with Gary, he said he wanted to talk through a tough decision he needed to make. They were a US-based company and they'd been presented with an expansion opportunity in another state. It was a huge project with a massive potential payoff for years to come. Despite that, he felt uneasy, as he knew he'd have to reallocate the team and resources to make it happen. He'd also need to commit to regular travel and time away from his family, which he didn't want to do. In his gut, the whole project felt out of alignment with their vision and what they were trying to achieve. But with so much money on the table, it was a tough call, as it's never easy to walk away from financial gains. As we discussed it further, it was clear that this opportunity also brought with it a huge amount of risk. Deep down Gary knew it was just a distraction and that they could drive more growth if they just stayed focused on what they were doing. Even more so if he put the energy and resources into other projects in their pipeline that were more aligned with the strategic direction they'd previously set. In the end, it was clear that he needed to say no. This took a huge weight off of him and he said that if we stopped right there, then helping him make that decision alone was worth the investment in working together.

The key to avoiding shiny objects is knowing what your goals and priorities are, then using that to guide the choices you make. This is even more important as a CEO, as you are going to be presented with new opportunities all the time. If you allow a scarcity mindset to cause you to act on emotion, then you'll constantly be chasing things you shouldn't due to fear of missing out. When you act in alignment with your vision though, it becomes easier to determine what's worth taking on.

I saw this happen with Lewis. In the time we'd worked together, he'd cut down his hours from 60 to 35 hours a week. He'd delegated everything he needed to, empowered the team and grown the business from doing six to seven figures a month. Everything was moving in the right direction and now it was vital to stay the course, as shifting focus could jeopardize growth. But being an entrepreneur, Lewis had also spotted an opening in the market. It was for a product within their industry that he believed would explode in the next five years. Meaning acting on this now *could* make them a leader in the market *if* it gained traction. In the past, he would have allowed the excitement to take over and he'd make this his main priority. Knowing that, we figured out what his core commitments and responsibilities were in the main business each week and how much time he needed for them. This allowed him to see that he had five hours available which he could use to focus on this new endeavor. This would be sufficient to explore this opportunity and see if there was merit in pursuing it at a higher degree. He'd also take time each week to reflect and ensure that doing so wasn't coming at the expense of the main business. In the end, he realized that this new opportunity wasn't a viable path and instead, it was simply a shiny object that seemed exciting. By being highly aware and intentional about his actions, he was able to stop wasting time on an endeavor that wouldn't pay off.

This is why you have to be brutally honest with yourself whenever you get new ideas as to whether or not they're something you can or should take on. Remember, great ideas and opportunities come and go all the time and very few are *the once-in-a-lifetime chances* that you convince yourself they are. Because of that, whenever you are presented with a new opportunity be honest with yourself: Is this *actually* a great idea? Is this aligned with your vision, business and what you are trying to achieve? Or is this a shiny object that is a potential distraction or something you want due to a scarcity mindset or feeling that you're missing out? Figure that out and it will become easier to decide whether or not this is something you should, or even have time to pursue.

There will however be situations where you do get great ideas, yet they just aren't aligned to your current goals or priorities right now. In those cases, I've got a simple solution I like to use to keep track of all of these, so that you can come back to them down the line.

Creating an *idea bank*

Whenever I get new ideas that I don't have time for right now, I place them in an *idea bank*. This is essentially a spreadsheet with two columns. On the one side, you place the idea, which could be anything from new campaigns to projects, hires, ventures or anything else you want to pursue. On the other side, you put all of the thoughts, insights or information you have about it.

This allows you to get the ideas out of your head and bank them, so you can free up your bandwidth and stop thinking about them. This is effective as you'll be able to do so without worrying that you'll forget any key points or thoughts. Then, when it comes time to set new goals or targets, you can go back through this list and see if anything is aligned with what you are aiming to achieve next.

The example I always give to clients about this is one of my own, from one January a few years ago. At the time I had a host of ideas of what I wanted to do that year, from writing a new book to launching a new podcast, a YouTube show and various other campaigns. While they all seemed exciting, I simply didn't have the time to do everything. Knowing my time was limited, I sat down and figured out my 90-day targets and what I wanted to achieve. Then I looked at which of these ideas were in alignment and would get me closer to where I wanted to be. Everything else was then dumped in the *idea bank* for me to revisit at a later date. Then, either every quarter or after every big project, I set new targets, reassessed my past ideas and aligned my focus from there.

Putting this all together

We've covered a lot so far, so to summarize this first part of the book, this is what you need to do:

1) Figure out your zone of genius, where your time has the greatest impact and what can only be done by you.
2) Audit the past to figure out where you've been spending your time and what you need to stop doing going forward.
3) Audit the future to see what you have coming up and identify what you shouldn't be involved in.
4) Every week, audit your tasks to see what you should be doing, what you need to delegate or get off your plate.

When doing the weekly audit, you need to go through each item and ask yourself:

1) Is this actually important? As in, will getting it done have a positive ROI, drive growth or impact the business? If no, remove it.
2) Is this a priority right now? Does it align with your 90-day goals and targets and do you have the energy and bandwidth to commit to this? If no, remove it from your list and set it aside for a later date.
3) If yes, does it need to be done by you?
4) If no, who could or should take over?

Doing this should be the first thing you do before starting any planning. It shouldn't take long and the few minutes you spend here could save you hours every week. It can also remove a lot of the anxiety and stress that comes with stretching yourself thin and overloading yourself.

You may now be in a situation where you know you need to delegate certain tasks, but internally you feel resistance to letting go. In the next section, we'll dive into effective delegation, keeping people accountable and ensuring people follow through, so that you can implement what you've learned so far.

Section 2

Effective Delegation

If you want to build a business that continues to grow and impacts the world, then a huge contributing factor to your success is going to be effective delegation, empowering your team and bringing out the best in those around you. After all, great companies aren't built by one person, but rather by a group of people coming together and working towards a common goal.

Yet, every week, I speak to CEOs who know they need to delegate more, but despite that, they struggle to let go. Now, the reasons range from being worried people will make mistakes, to convincing themselves that no one will do it as well as them or that it's quicker just to do it themselves. Many also don't know what they should be delegating or even worry that other people are busy and they don't want to overload them. These are all legitimate concerns and I completely understand and empathize with wanting to uphold your standards and ensure things are done correctly. Especially when you're emotionally invested, as the company is such a big part of your life, or your reputation is on the line. As you've seen so far in this book though, all holding on is going to do is leave you stretched thin and overwhelmed. Not only that, but everything you do has a cost, meaning every hour you spend on one thing will come at the expense of something else.

That's why if you want to be a highly effective CEO, we have to make you more defensive with your time. One of the best ways to do that? Effectively delegate and get tasks off your plate. I know it may be scary, but if you want to get to the next level without burning out or losing your sanity, then this is part of the role you have to embrace. That doesn't mean being reckless, but it does mean slowing down, clearly communicating expectations and holding people accountable. When you get that right, that's when you can get out of the weeds and free yourself up to focus on your real priorities.

Why you struggle with delegation

Generally, when someone struggles with delegation it's because they worry the team (or person) can't do it, and either they haven't allowed them to step up, or when they have, the job hadn't been completed well enough or to the standard expected.

If it's a skill and people problem, then that's a foundational issue and you may need to revisit your hiring practices or even replace and reorganize the team. I'll regularly have conversations with CEOs who either know in their gut or have enough evidence to see that someone isn't going to be able to deliver on a task or job. In these cases, it's on you to correct and deal with the underperformance.

However, part of delegation is also coming to terms with the fact that people will make mistakes. It's inevitable and something that needs to happen for them to get better professionally. Making a mistake doesn't necessarily mean they can't or won't be able to fulfill it. They may just need time, guidance and the opportunity to figure out what needs to get done. Because of that, it's on you as a leader to create an environment where they feel comfortable navigating and completing their tasks. Also, there is likely more than one way to do a task, so at times, you may need to be at peace with the fact that someone may not approach things exactly like you would. Ultimately, what matters is the outcome and results. Yet I've seen so many CEOs get stuck in a perfectionist mindset, causing them to obsess over details that don't actually matter.

To set your team up for success, you need to be highly intentional with how you communicate expectations to help them understand what needs to get done. You also need to keep them accountable to ensure they follow through. These are the soft skills that I find a lot of leaders struggle with, especially those who have stepped into or been thrown into the role.

Aaron was a perfect example of this. When we first started working together, he came to one session frustrated that he'd delegated a project to his team, but when they presented it back to him, they completely missed the mark. The final piece of work was completely different to what he had told them he wanted and Aaron was really starting to question their competence and whether he'd hired the right people. Now, it's completely possible that someone may not be cut out for a task, but whenever there is more than one underperformer involved in a negative outcome, it's usually a red flag that the CEO (or manager/person in charge) hasn't done a good job in communicating what is required.

I told Aaron to go back to the team and get them to talk him through their thinking and why they approached the project the way they did. Once he had this kind of context, he completely understood how his team came to that solution, as his miscommunication meant they completely misunderstood what outcome he was after in the first place.

I find that when you're a founder, entrepreneur or visionary thinker, you're used to executing and operating at pace. In fact, this is probably how you've built a lot of your momentum and traction in the past, as you had an idea, knew what you needed to do and dived in. While this approach may have worked when you were driving the execution, with a growing team, operating this way can be catastrophic for long-term success. After all, people can't read your mind. So, just because something makes sense to you, doesn't mean it makes sense to everyone else. You've got to remember, as the one setting the direction, that you have so much added context, a clearer vision and information that other people simply don't. To make matters worse, if you rush explaining it to them, bounce around between ideas or quickly move on to the next thing, you are going to leave them overwhelmed or confused.

That's why it's so important to recognize that effective leadership is not about rushing ahead and hoping people catch up. Instead, it's about taking them along the ride with you. Sure, it may feel unnatural and take longer, but if you want to avoid future headaches and mistakes, then you have to slow down and ensure people are on the same page as you before moving on.

How to communicate expectations

I've seen a pattern among leaders where they allow their enthusiasm for a project to cause them to bounce around between ideas or go off on tangents when sharing them with everyone else. This confuses people, making it hard to decipher what is actually important or needs to be accomplished. Because of that, the first thing you need to do is figure out what point you *need* to get across. Think about the outcome you want. What would make this task or project a success? What do you know that other people don't? What could they get wrong or misunderstand?

By taking the time to figure this all out, it'll be far easier to create a plan, structure and brief for what you need your team to achieve. Then it's on you to talk someone through it, making sure you communicate everything they need to know. A key part of getting this right will be staying on point. Especially in moments when new ideas pop into your head, as you've got to resist the urge to divert the focus.

Jason was massively guilty of this. He'd grown the company from just him to a team of 35+, but one of the biggest challenges was getting them to meet the same quality and standard of work he met when he did it all himself. Their company deals with a lot of data and they have incredibly complex structures in place as part of the work they do for clients. What Jason kept finding was that he'd delegate a task, then a few weeks down the line, he'd see there were a tonne of mistakes. This would cause him to get pulled back in, often requiring 10 to 15 hours of his time to fix it. This was happening with multiple members of his team, so I knew something was off in how he was communicating and setting expectations. I got Jason to talk me through his process and it became clear that while he was telling people what to do, he'd often derail his main story, and introduce new ideas of things they could do in the future, completely bombarding the person with information. When sharing, it made sense to him, but it left others completely overwhelmed. For whatever reason, his team didn't speak up, they just said it all made sense then they'd go away and try to figure it out on their own.

To get this under control, he had to slow down. He needed to plan in advance exactly what was needed for the brief and to clearly communicate to the team what they had to do. He also had to consciously stop himself from going off course, as just because new ideas came into his head that excited him, didn't mean he needed to share them. Not straight away and especially not when briefing the team on the current project or task.

Then, instead of just assuming someone understood the assignment, I suggested saying to them "Talk me through exactly what you need to do". The reason this was so effective was because it helped Jason find the gaps in his own communication. If someone couldn't explain it back, then the task was still unclear. That, for him, would be the sign that he hadn't done a good enough job of communicating what was required. By doing so he could go back, rephrase and reframe his thoughts, answer any questions and ensure his team had everything they needed to do a great job.

The extra few minutes he spent here reduced the majority of headaches and mistakes, meaning he was no longer being pulled back into tasks. This allowed him to start spending the bulk of his time operating in his zone of genius and working on the business. It also proved to him that his team was highly capable, they just needed the right guidance stemming from clear communication and expectations.

To do this yourself, you have to get clear on exactly what you want and share that vision or requirement in a way that everyone can understand what good looks like. This is how you can ensure that the entire room is on the same page as you. Then, rather than just assuming that people know what to do, slow down, ask the right questions and ensure your team has what they need to make headway on said project or task.

Keeping people accountable

The other part of delegation people tend to miss is the accountability factor. Many leaders (especially newer ones) struggle with the idea of holding people to what they need to do. I've even heard from various clients about how when they were working their way up in their career, they always kept on top of things and hit deadlines without anyone watching over them. Because of that, they didn't see why other people needed accountability in the first place. The reality is though that not everyone is a self-starter, or has the same mindset, ability or standards. This is why as a leader and high performer, not recognizing that people operate differently risks setting you up for disappointment, frustration and failure.

Not only that, but the right people thrive on accountability. Meaning that not holding people accountable is doing them, the organization and yourself a disservice. That's why if you want to be an effective CEO, you have to accept that keeping people accountable is not hand-holding - your team is still expected to deliver their work without you getting involved in the small stuff. Nor is it micromanaging, nagging or saying you don't trust them. Instead, it's adding checks and balances that will enable them to perform at their best. It also helps them get clear on what is needed and expected of them. This is key, as someone can't improve if they don't know what they should be doing or that something is wrong.

On one of our coaching calls, Tom told me how frustrated he was that 10 days ago he delegated a task to someone and he found out they'd only completed it that morning. Getting it done only took a couple of hours and he said that if he knew they'd take that long he'd have just done it himself. He'd done well in delegating, but I asked him "Did you tell them when you needed it by?" He said no. What I had to remind Tom was that he'd already told me how busy his team was. Since he didn't make it clear that this task was a priority, then it's likely it just got added to their to-do list.

When delegating tasks, it's important that you set a clear expectation about deadlines. By giving someone a cut-off point they will then have an easier time organizing their work and priorities. It also means that if someone keeps dropping the ball, then you can escalate the issue and investigate why they aren't following through. This is where status and feedback processes come into place, as they can be essential to ensure people are on track to hit deadlines and get done what they need to do.

Status and feedback loops

When Sarah and I met, one of her biggest challenges was getting people to follow through. She'd delegate tasks and hand items off, then they'd either not get done or come back filled with issues and mistakes. This meant that she was constantly being dragged back into the day-to-day, at the expense of the top-level work that could only be done by her. From our conversations, it was clear that the huge issue she was having was with keeping people accountable. In addition, the many competing priorities and moving parts also made it hard for her to keep track of what and when items were due. I suggested implementing a tracking, status and feedback process to keep on top of everything. In its simplest form, this was a spreadsheet where new tasks were added along with what needed to be done, who it needed to be done by and when it needed to be completed. Having this in place meant she could easily see exactly what was outstanding, but there was no need for her to spend time on this. Instead, Sarah delegated the ownership of the project tracker to her rockstar assistant, who'd add new tasks to the list at her request, oversee the day-to-day timeline and chase people for updates. For instance, if something was due next Thursday, then on Tuesday she'd contact them to ensure that it would be done on time. This new measure was a game changer for Sarah as it meant her team started hitting deadlines instead of missing them.

The benefit of having the correct status update processes is they can also allow you to see the progress of certain projects along the way without being directly involved in them. They also enable you to then intervene as and when necessary. For instance, with larger projects, Sarah and her team agreed on having specific milestones where she'd need to see the work, such as sign-off stages. Here she could ask any questions or add her insights and together they could agree on the next actions and steps. This again allowed her to get out of the cycle of seeing something a few weeks down the line, only to realize the team was off course or out of alignment. Having this in place also meant she could ensure progress was being made without having to micromanage or be overinvolved.

That's why having status and feedback processes are so important, as they can ensure that everyone is operating on the same page. Now, your situation may be different. Maybe you have a smaller team, or you don't have a rockstar assistant in your corner. That doesn't mean you can't implement accountability practices. Yes, it may mean you need more structure and to be more organized, but whenever you delegate tasks (especially larger ones) think about what you need in place to ensure people follow through. What are the deadlines? What intervals do you need to be updated at? What would allow you to feel at ease and not worry about what is going on? Figure that out and you'll have a much easier time staying on top of what's going on.

Having these processes becomes even more essential as your company grows and your team expands. Even more so in situations where time constraints will mean you have less frequent or direct access to your team.

Someone who found out the hard way the consequences of not having this in place was Jerry. He is the CEO of a company that has massively grown over the last few years. Now, between all the responsibilities, stakeholders to keep happy and other challenges that came with his role, he barely had time to keep tabs on what was happening across the business. This meant he'd regularly find himself in situations where he'd get pulled into problems several weeks after they started or once they'd become massive issues. The frustrating part was that if he'd known about them a few weeks prior, he would have been able to intervene or support to mitigate the problem or reduce its impact.

He didn't want to add more meetings with every department to stay updated with projects and progress. Instead, what I got him to do was create a status and feedback process which came in the form of a twice-weekly check-in report that was sent to him by the head of every department (ranging from ops to marketing, sales, HR, finance, etc.). Monday focused on the intention of the week, including their priorities and targets. Friday served as a recap of the week, including the progress that was made, challenges that came up and anything else Jerry needed to be aware of. The five minutes he'd take to read these on a Monday and Friday would then allow him to have a bird's eye view of what was going on in the company. From there, he knew where he needed to get involved, the status of projects and everything else that was happening on a macro level. This status update also made it easier to hold people accountable, as managers knew they had to report on what was happening. In turn, these managers were keeping on top of their teams' progress, thus creating a trickle-down effect that held everyone accountable throughout the organization. Not only did this allow Jerry to feel more in control, it also removed a lot of anxiety and stress that previously came from either being pulled into big problems or worrying about what could be going wrong.

While this worked for Jerry, in many situations a twice-a-week report will be overkill. With other clients, we've implemented a single report once a week that wrapped up the progress from the previous week *and* that set the focus for the next. This single report was sufficient and better suited for the pace of the company and people's workloads. This is why how you implement practices like this will depend on you, your company, your team size, the information you need and a variety of other factors. The key thing to figure out is what information you require to stay in the loop. That in itself comes from proper preparation, where before you delegate or have meetings, you are clear on the outcome and the view you need. It also helps to look at the company on the whole, what is causing bottlenecks, stalling progress or causing anxiety and stress. Uncover that, and you can start to look at what you need to have in place to reduce your headaches and problems.

Buying back time

I find that one of the biggest barriers stopping people from delegating is dealing with the reality that they are spending money on something they could or usually do themselves. I've seen it so many times where CEOs get stuck in a scarcity mindset, justifying to themselves all the reasons they can't let someone else deliver a task or project. Sure, in some situations this is understandable, especially when cash is tight, or their runway is limited. In others though, it's simply a mental barrier caused by focusing on what they need to give up, instead of what they have to gain by getting out of these tasks.

To help put you at ease with any potential future expenditure, I've got a simple exercise that you can do to put the situation into perspective. The first thing you need to do is figure out roughly how much an hour of your time is worth. As in, if you did an hour of focused work, how much revenue could you drive or how much growth could you create in the company?

To keep it simple, let's say an hour of your time is worth $1,000 dollars. In this situation, you should not be doing tasks that you could pay someone else $30 an hour to do, because every hour you spend on those tasks is costing the business $970. Knowing this makes it easier to justify the expense, as you can assign values to certain tasks and responsibilities and use that to determine where you need to remove yourself.

Sometimes it's not just the monetary side that's important, as certain tasks can also drain your energy and focus, making you less effective in other things you need to get done. I went through a situation that involved both of these aspects during the launch of my previous book. For the campaign, there was a huge amount that needed to be done. A big part of our strategy was leveraging podcasts and influencers to promote the launch. Organizing both of these was a time-consuming and arduous task, as it required extensive research, outreach, vetting and coordinating. I'd done both in the past, so I knew what was needed, but after two days of trying to do it all myself, I was mentally drained, bored and exhausted. With everything else I had to get done for the launch, I recognized that there was no way I could keep this up and get everything else done while keeping my energy up and sanity intact. Because of that, I hired an assistant to help with the podcasts, PR and other everyday tasks. I also hired someone else to run the influencer campaign.

I was paying for this campaign out of my own pocket, which is why I completely understand why people are reluctant to let go when it's something they need to fund themselves. I knew though that if I wanted the launch to be a success, as well as get through it without burning out or going insane, then I needed help. This is why it's so important to look at the bigger picture, as I also knew that with all the time saved, I could easily make all the costs back and more by using that time intentionally elsewhere in the business.

This is why I'm a big believer in buying back time, where you look holistically at your life and all the things that are taking you away from what you want or need to do. Then wherever possible, if freeing yourself up can make you more money, reduce stress or give you a better quality of life, then it's often worth making it happen.

With one client, after being promoted to an executive position, she found herself working long days to keep up with all the responsibilities that came with the role. That meant by the time she got home, had dinner, sorted the kitchen and got her life together, she barely had any time for her family or herself. Knowing that, she arranged for a cleaner to come in an hour a day to keep everything in order (like cleaning the kitchen and tidying up). This essentially allowed her to buy back that hour with her family each night, which to her, more than justified the expense. I've had other clients hire chefs to take care of meals, VAs to get rid of admin work and even personal assistants to deal with their life tasks. Essentially, they figured out what drained their energy, what they were struggling to get around to or didn't want to do, then outsourced it accordingly.

Think about what you are doing or taking on that isn't a good use of your days, and from there, what could you do to buy back that time? Getting this right is going to go a long way to helping you take control of your life and business.

What if you can't delegate it yet?

You may find yourself in situations where you know you should be and want to delegate certain tasks, but either it's just not feasible right now, or there is too much risk. I'll give you three examples of different scenarios along with how I advised clients to handle them.

Earlier I told you about Adam who I got to create a list of tasks he needed to do and he came back to me with a list of 46 items. Part of the work we were doing was focused on getting him out of working in the business so that he could work on it instead. There was one task in particular that was taking around eight hours a month to do. It involved a detailed report containing data and financial metrics breaking down the work they'd done for one of their customers. Now, this customer was responsible for 80% of their revenue, so understandably Adam had huge fears about letting this go. Especially since losing that customer could mean their whole business would go under. Telling him to *just let it go* and not worry would have been terrible advice, as there was a real risk, and mistakes could have huge consequences.

Rather than letting it go straight away, I suggested a staggered approach. He figured out who would be the best person to take over this report, and he trained them on what needed to be done. Then, because so much depended on getting this right, he also taught a second person, who would be responsible for checking their work. Finally, Adam would then sign-off on the final version, before it was sent to the client. We agreed that he'd continue being the final sign off until the report hit his desk with no mistakes three consecutive times. At that point, he'd trust that his team had it handled.

Approaching it this way allowed him to give the team the guidance and support to learn what to do. It also stopped him from being an anxious wreck, since the team proved to him that they were more than capable of delivering the work correctly. Luckily for Adam, he had great people around him who picked it up straight away. So instead of this being a drawn-out process, after three months he was comfortable with no longer being involved.

Tony had a financial background, so when his CFO left, it was only natural that he stepped in to oversee that role until a replacement was found. It took several weeks, but after interviewing numerous candidates he found the perfect replacement. Just like any new hire though, she needed time to get to know the business and settle into the role. Because of that, Tony couldn't simply hand over the financial responsibilities to his new CFO all at once. Instead, we mapped out a transition plan where as she settled in, she'd slowly take over projects. While this kept Tony in tasks he didn't want to do for a bit longer, he could also see the light at the end of the tunnel for when he could let them go.

Sam was a COO turned CEO, who'd stepped into the role of running a scale-up. While business was growing, their runway was short and they had various financial challenges that prevented her from making any huge hires. One thing she desperately wanted was a competent COO, as with her background, she found herself doing two roles. This hire simply wasn't possible right now, so we figured out what revenue the business needed to get to for her to justify the expense. Knowing that, she then set clear targets and actively found ways to include the hire in the next budget.

From all of these, you can see how for these CEOs, it wasn't simply a case of knowing they should delegate and let go. Instead, leaders often find themselves having to work within the constraints of the situation they are in. The key thing with all of the three CEOs above was that they all identified what or *who* they needed, a realistic time frame and what would need to align to make it happen. By doing so, they were able to be highly intentional with their plans moving forward.

Removing yourself from the business

A lot of the clients I work with started a business because they wanted to set their own hours, be their own boss and live a life of freedom on their terms. Yet between all the firefighting, solving other people's problems and never-ending demands, the company has essentially taken over their life and can't function without them in it. This is where effective delegation, status updates, feedback loops and accountability come into play, as they are the things you need to get the business to run without you. I'll give you some examples of this in action, so that you can get some ideas as to how you too could remove yourself from your business (or at least reduce its reliance on you).

Angela had built a thriving service-based business. She'd started it with just her, a laptop and a phone, and now they were a team of over 40 doing close to eight figures in revenue a year. While she'd done an amazing job building the company, the industry was highly reactive, with problems coming out of nowhere and customers needing immediate resolutions and assistance. To make matters worse, everything depended on her, meaning she was deeply involved in every area of the business. It was exhausting and she was regularly working 12 to 14 hour days just to keep everything running.

She hired me because she wanted help getting out of the daily grind. She wanted to have freedom, to enjoy life and to start doing all the things she'd been putting off. Her biggest goal was to take a month off for her and her husband to travel and go on a golf holiday. But with how busy she was, she simply didn't think it would ever be possible to step away for a week, let alone a month. Especially since anytime she'd taken time off in the past, she'd spent half the time on her phone, with people calling her to ask questions and needing assistance.

I took her through exactly what this book is all about, figuring out what she *should* be doing and implementing ways to defend her time. We also focused heavily on setting boundaries, getting people to solve their own problems and preventing the team from just dumping everything on her desk. This allowed her to successfully take back control of her time. Instead of working until 10 pm and having dinner at her office desk, she was able to start leaving at 6 pm, making it home for dinner and she was even able to start attending a few fitness classes a week. Once the team started taking more ownership, the next goal became to finish early on a Friday. She signed up for golf lessons and committed to leaving at 1 pm. To ensure this was possible, she communicated to the team that if they needed anything, it had to be dealt with before that time.

After that was running smoothly, we set our sights on that month off and she booked the summer trip, which was five months away. That gave us plenty of time to get the office in order. We started to reverse engineer the journey, thinking about what other people needed to do or take over, for her to be away for a month (and not stress about it). Figuring this out gave us a clear plan of what had to be delegated. With the time frame in mind, we used a staggered approach. For the first three months, she'd slowly let go, while still giving guidance wherever it was needed. Then for the final two months, she removed herself completely. This approach allowed her to feel at ease, as she had proof that the team could handle her tasks. It also meant that instead of throwing them into the deep end, she was on hand to support them while they got up to speed.

This highly intentional approach ultimately empowered her team to take these tasks off her plate. This meant that she could go on her trip without the fear that everything would fall apart, because her business was running without her (the ultimate goal for any leader or founder looking for a work-life balance). The added bonus came when she returned. Now that she was no longer involved in everything, she could allocate her time to her zone of genius, which for Angela, was business development, in turn, allowing them to continue to scale.

Alan was in a similar situation, where as a founder turned CEO, he was heavily involved in every area of the business. As they were a global company, that meant he was often working from the moment he woke up to 10 pm handling issues across a variety of time zones.

To get him out of the trenches, we approached the process in the same way, figuring out what would need to happen to free him up from his everyday tasks. Fast forward a few months and he'd gone from 60+ hour weeks to only having leadership meetings on a Monday and update meetings with the rest of the team on Tuesdays and Thursdays. This has allowed him to take the whole of Wednesday off to do charity work, go on adventures with his wife or simply spend the time doing what he wanted to do. He's also only working half-day Fridays from the gym, where he takes a few calls and just ensures everything is in order. What this has allowed him to do is shift his role from being integral in the day-to-day, to being the overseer and strategic lead. Not only has this given him the freedom to live the life he imagined when he started his company, it also furthered his future ambitions of exiting the business in the next 12 to 24 months. The reason being is he's now proven it can both run and grow without him, making it far more attractive to potential buyers.

When it comes to removing yourself from working in the business, it doesn't need to be this extreme. Not all founders-turned-CEOs want to exit and not all want to work four days a week. For Grant, he wanted to take a week off to go on a fishing trip with his dad and brother. The thought was terrifying as he was worried about what will go wrong without him being there. Knowing the trip was in four weeks, we first figured out what needed to be covered in his absence. Then he communicated this to the team and asked them what they'd need to handle these tasks without him. From there, they worked out a phased approach, similar to Angela's case above. This gave Grant and his team time to test the waters, ask questions and ensure they had it covered before he went away. Meaning they were confident in what to do, and he could go and enjoy the time with his family.

With all of these examples, the reason Angela, Alan and Grant were able to step away is because we worked on being highly intentional with what they needed to delegate and let go of. So, whether you are looking for ways to remove yourself for a week, month or even long-term, you have to reverse engineer what needs to be in place to enable you to do that confidently. Look at your existing tasks and think who could take over. Then have the conversations, tell people the time frame in which you need them to take ownership and support them accordingly. You may even need to factor this in for your next hires to ensure they have the skill sets to handle certain areas of your role. This is how you can break the shackles that often come with running a company. One thing you will notice with all of these examples is they were all entrepreneurs and founders turned CEOs. I've found that they're generally more ingrained in the business, especially if they built and scaled it from a small team. They also tend to be more emotionally invested, making it harder to let go, take time off and they face more anxiety over everything falling apart without them. If you're an entrepreneur or founder, then regardless of what stage you're at, it can help to start being intentional with how you are going to get out of the trenches down the line. That can help massively with the decisions you make along the way, especially in terms of processes and new hires.

Obviously, in order for any of this to work, you have to ensure you surround yourself with the right team. But if you've done your job in attracting great people, then there's no reason why you can't start actively focusing on allowing them to take over some of your responsibilities.

When delegation goes too far

This section has been heavily focused on delegation and freeing you up to do the things you want or need to do. I have in the past seen CEOs take this too far, where as a result, they make themselves miserable. This was the situation James found himself in. His background was being an engineer and in the beginning, he had primarily been focused on product development. But after scaling the company and stepping into the role of CEO, he'd handed off all of these responsibilities, as instead, he believed all his time needed to be spent on driving revenue and growing the company.

His intentions and thinking were all in the right place, as he'd figured out what he needed to do and what had a negative ROI on his time, then delegated accordingly. This made even more sense as he had an incredible team of engineers who had all their product development handled. The problem though was all the endless meetings, tough conversations and tasks had made him start to resent the business. So much so, that he was starting to question whether or not the daily firefighting and pressure was actually worth it, given the lack of excitement, fun and fulfillment.

The problem for James was that he had honed his focus so much that he'd lost sight of why he started the company in the first place. This is why I suggested that he allow himself to spend a few hours each week in the lab playing around with tech and contributing to product development. On paper, this was a terrible use of his time. However, this reignited his inner passion and he once again got excited for what they were doing. This shift in headspace made it much easier to deal with all the other challenges he faced each day. Since then, he's made this a non-negotiable part of his week.

The moral of the story is that yes, as you scale you do want to let go of tasks that shouldn't be done by you. But just make sure you don't go so far that you take out the things that actually make you want to get out of bed in the morning. Because if you're excited by what you are doing, then it's so much easier to show up, take action and push the business to new heights of success.

Putting this all together

The reality is that highly effective CEOs are leaders who are able to get more done by getting other people to think for themselves. To free yourself up to do more of what matters, you need to:

1) Determine what you need to delegate and get off your plate.
2) Figure out the outcome you want, what people need to know and also consider what context or information you have that they don't.
3) Focus on clearly communicating what is required, staying on point and slowing down to ensure everyone understands the goal.
4) Make sure everyone is on the same page and agree to deadlines, next steps and accountability.
5) Where necessary, implement status updates to keep you in the loop.

Get this right and you'll be able to build a company that runs smoothly, where people feel empowered and consistently follow through. One thing to note is that for any of this to work, you have to accept that people will make mistakes. It's part of life and it's unavoidable. It's why some CEOs implemented phased approaches to their delegation, as this gave everyone the safe space needed to learn. Now, there are limits to that and there will be times you need to intervene or accept that someone isn't cut out for the role. But instead of just assuming that to be the case, you have to give people the opportunity to step up and trust that you (or those around you) did a good job in hiring the right team. I know it's not easy, but the alternative is that you continue to do everything yourself.

Section 3

Energy Management

Let's be honest, running a business can be exhausting. Especially when you add in the long hours, huge pressure, endless demands and the sheer amount of time and effort it takes to create (and sustain) momentum and growth. That's why a huge contributing factor to your long-term success is going to be your ability to stay energized and focused. Yet I regularly speak to CEOs who are burnt out and exhausted. Often this is because they've been pushing themselves to the limit, where inevitably their business takes its toll mentally, physically and emotionally.

I saw this happen on a coaching application call with Leo. I'd seen him on LinkedIn and all the recognition his company was getting from winning numerous awards. From the outside, it was all smiles and it looked like everything was going great. When we got on the call, it quickly became clear that the social media façade was nowhere close to his reality. He told me about how over the last 18 months they'd doubled in size and after just securing a new fund raise, they were about to do it again. He was exhausted. His marriage had broken down. He wasn't around for his kids. It had been months since he'd exercised or had a decent night's sleep. It had taken everything out of him to get to this point and he didn't know if he had any fight left in him to do it again. Yet with so many people counting on him, every morning he'd pick himself up, put on a brave face and carry on. It was clear to him his situation wasn't working, but with so much on the line, he felt backed into a corner, with no choice but to push through.

I've felt that way myself, so I know how it feels to be constantly exhausted and low on energy to the point you struggle to just get through the day. There was even a period in building my business where I felt like a zombie, drifting through life. I remember getting so used to feeling low on energy, that I'd forgotten what it actually felt like to feel good.

During this period, I had such severe brain fog, that at times just doing everyday tasks was a challenge. I'd struggle to focus, have difficulty concentrating and I'd constantly lose my train of thought. Like when I was reading something and I'd struggle to make sense of it or I'd forget what happened in the last paragraph, so I'd have to start again. This made it incredibly hard to think and make decisions, and I'd regularly have days where I wanted nothing more than to just lie on the couch in my office to try and get some sleep. But with so much to do, people counting on me and responsibilities I had to deliver on, I kept telling myself that I couldn't afford to slow down.

One day I went to visit my parents for coffee. I'd driven the way home hundreds of times, but on that day, I felt completely disorientated to the point I couldn't remember if I'd missed my exit. Recently I had been forgetful and struggled to remember things, but this was the first big warning sign about how bad it had gotten. Honestly, it was terrifying, and I remember saying to my partner that night that I was starting to get scared that something was severely wrong and that I'd end up in the hospital. Later that week I went to the doctor, got full blood work done and extensive tests to figure out why I was constantly low on energy and fatigued. It all came back clear with a clean bill of health, which was further proof that the way I felt was because I was stressed out of my mind.

What you need to understand about burnout and brain fog is it's all lifestyle-related. It happens from not looking after yourself, not exercising, not eating right, not getting enough high-quality sleep and being under huge amounts of stress. It also doesn't happen overnight. Instead, it's the compounding effect of months or years of neglecting your wellbeing. Because of that, there's no miracle cure and it takes time to heal. One of the harsh lessons I've learned is that if you don't make time to look after yourself, there will come a day when you have no choice but to do it. I saw this with one client who, on our introductory call, told me he had pushed himself so hard that the doctor had booked him off for 10 weeks with the order to rest and recover.

Part of the problem is that as high performers, we tend to want to do everything as fast as possible. Combine that with the standards and expectations we have for ourselves, and so much of the pressure we are under is because we put it there. The thing is though, building and running a company is a marathon, not a race. This is why if you want to thrive and not just survive, you have to approach it accordingly.

To keep this under control, I've had to become highly intentional with the habits, behaviors and routines that I stick to so that I can ensure I protect my health, energy and mental wellbeing. It's also why this is a big part of the work I do with clients, as in order to help them show up as the leader their business needs, it's essential that they feel their best inside and out. After all, the way you feel is going to directly impact everything from your focus to your decision-making, your productivity, your ability to control your emotions and so much more.

Over the years I've tested, discovered and developed various frameworks and strategies to help people make this happen. In this section, I'm going to take you through some of these and show you how you can implement them yourself. The best part about these is that they work regardless of whether you are burnt out and need to recover, or if you want to use them preventatively to avoid getting to that point. I'm taking you through these strategies now, because when we get to the Effective Planning section later in this book, you'll then be able to keep them top of mind when you start to structure your days and weeks.

Push and pull days

When it comes to daily routines, I find that people tend to try and approach every day the same. They get up at the same time. Take the same actions and generally try to stay consistent with what they do. Sure, this is better than nothing, but from a high-performance standpoint, it's far from optimal, as it doesn't factor in the variety you have in your days and the tasks and milestones each brings.

That's why when it comes to energy management, my favorite strategy to incorporate is the concept of *push and pull days*. A *push* day is a day where you go all out. You wake up early, work hard, maybe put in more hours and take on more focus-intensive tasks. A *pull* day is when you allow yourself to step back and recover. You lighten your workload, take on tasks that require less bandwidth and allow yourself to recharge.

I find that overwhelmed CEOs tend to focus too much on *push* days. Over an extended period of time, this approach simply isn't sustainable, as it leads to burnout and overall performance suffering. That's why both of these types of days are vital, and they need to be both scheduled, as well as easily implemented when needed. I'll give you a few examples of this in action.

When Mark came to me, he was absolutely crushing Monday and Tuesday. He'd spring out of bed fired up, energized and ready to attack the week ahead. By Wednesday though, his energy would start to fade and he was nowhere near as focused or productive. This slump would get worse on Thursday, and Friday was pretty much a write-off. What I found was that he was pushing so hard on Monday and Tuesday that he depleted his energy tank, leaving him running on fumes for the rest of the week. Then he'd refuel on the weekend, only to be in the same cycle again week after week.

I encouraged Mark to implement a *pull* day on Wednesdays. That meant allowing himself to sleep in and not scheduling any stressful meetings or high-bandwidth tasks. I also suggested blocking off his calendar after 3 pm so that he could hit the gym, play tennis, get a massage, or do anything else he felt like doing.

At first, he was highly resistant to the idea, telling me how he needed to be working and that he had too much to do to "slack off". The thought alone of slowing down made him feel guilty, as he believed that as a CEO he should be doing more, not less. Despite his hesitation, I convinced him to just try it and see what happens. He found that by taking his foot off the accelerator on a Wednesday, he was able to recharge and recover. This allowed him to go into Thursday and Friday with the same level of energy that he had at the start of the week. In terms of output, he essentially went from having two highly productive days a week to four.

This setup however is not a one-size-fits-all approach. If I use myself as an example, I'm the complete opposite of Mark. For whatever reason, I find that Mondays are my least creative days of the week. That's why if I try to force tasks like writing, filming videos or anything that I need to be in a flow state for, I struggle. I also find that trying to push through has a negative impact on my focus and energy for the rest of the week. Instead, I treat Monday as a *pull* day. I sleep in, have a slower start to the morning and I generally fill the day with meetings and less intensive tasks. Doing so then allows me to wake up energized Tuesday to Thursday where I have time defended for when I feel on top of my game. From a zone of genius standpoint, I do all my writing and content creation in the mornings of these days, as it's when I feel the most in the zone.

To figure out what will work best for you, it's important to look objectively at your situation and your energy status throughout the week (and even based on the time of day). Because if you try to treat every day the same, you risk setting yourself up for failure. Allison was stuck in this trap. She'd recently taken a new position which required that two days a week she had to get the train into the city to work from the office. These days meant she had to get up early and she didn't get home until late. Despite that, she still had the best intentions to exercise and keep on top of her life tasks. Yet, she never did, thus beating herself up and feeling like she was failing. I got her to treat the days in the office as *push* days where she accepted that other priorities, such as exercising and life admin, would need to be set aside. Then, on the days she worked from home, she'd *pull* back, scheduling in time to work out and take care of any other non-work responsibilities. For *push* and *pull* days to work, you have to look at the bigger picture and accept that different days have different priorities, commitments, responsibilities and flows of energy. For Allison, reframing her to-do list through this lens was huge. It meant she could deprioritize some jobs on specific days, in order to focus on them at a different time. She'd achieve her weekly goals in a way that allowed her to succeed both at work and in her personal life, without feeling guilty for not ticking tasks off sooner.

Take some time to think about your average week. What days do you feel the most energized? When do you start to struggle? What throws you off your game? How could you incorporate the *push* and *pull* approach into your routine? By figuring this out, you can start to develop a structure that works for you.

The best thing about this approach is the pressure that you are able to take off yourself. Let's say you're tired and need to take a step back, it can be easier to do so without guilt when you recognize it's a *pull* day. Obviously, you need to be honest with yourself, as this is not an excuse to be lazy. Instead, it's a strategy built around longevity, allowing you to get more out of your weeks and years. There are also going to be situations where you can or may need to take this a step further. For instance, let's say next week you have a big launch and you know it's going to be intense with long hours and a lot of stress. Knowing that, you can intentionally *pull* back this week to ensure you are relaxed and come Monday, you'll be ready to hit the ground running. Also, I find that generally whenever people have a week that disrupts their routine, they tend to need a *pull* day to ease back into it. This holds true whether it's a business trip or vacation. This is why I always advise my clients to take the first morning back to work as a *pull* morning. That way they can use it to plan, strategize and get back in the zone.

Now, you may be reading all this and thinking it sounds good in theory, but you aren't sure whether or not this could work for you. That's what happened to Samuel. When I first took him through this approach, he was convinced this would never work for him. Not with all his responsibilities and him feeling like he was drowning in an ocean of things to do. The big goal we were working towards was reducing his work commitments to 30 hours a week. Once I got him defending his time, holding people accountable and out of the tasks he shouldn't be doing to begin with, he started to feel more in control of his days. This allowed him to start seeing and believing in a reality where the 30-hour week was possible and that strategies like this could work for him. Now that we got everything else in place, he's committed to taking a *pull* day on Wednesdays. He works from 9 until 12, then he has the afternoon blocked off to spend with his kids, taking them to their various events and sporting practices. He also does a half day on Friday so that he can finish early and play golf.

I share this as you may not be able to implement some of these concepts straight away. By becoming intentional about the life and business you want to create though, you can start introducing changes that will allow you to make them happen. This is another area where it helps to reverse engineer the results you want. Think about what needs to be different or what has to change in your current schedule or set up for that to be possible.

State of flow planning

When Lucas and I first started working together he'd taken a product to market, built a team and scaled his company. Now he was looking to take it to the next level and his biggest priority was to close their next round of funding. To make that happen he needed to spend the majority of his time writing proposals, creating presentations and pitching to potential investors.

On top of fundraising, he also had his regular responsibilities. To keep on top of everything, he followed the standard productivity advice of creating a to-do list and tackling the most important tasks first. This made sense, because why wouldn't you do the most important things first? While practices like this may work for your average person, they can be catastrophic for a CEO. The reason being is they can be short-sighted, often prioritizing what's vital *that day*, without factoring in your big-picture goals or targets.

That's exactly what was happening to Lucas and as a result, he spent most of his days putting out fires, solving other people's problems, attending meetings and dealing with administrative problems. This was a huge issue. If he was lucky, by 3 pm he'd maybe get an hour to focus on fundraising. Only by then, he was mentally drained and out of bandwidth. Meaning he was lacking the energy and creativity he needed to do these tasks effectively. To make matters worse, if he didn't close this round, they'd run out of runway and there wouldn't be day-to-day challenges to get pulled into to begin with.

I got him to gain clarity on how much time he needed each week for his top-level, high-value work, what state of energy and flow he needed to be in to make the most of it and what times of day he was most often in this state of flow. We figured he needed around 15 hours a week to focus on fundraising - his top-level, high-value tasks. He also worked best in the morning, as that's when he was energized and able to focus. Knowing that, I got him to block off his days from 9 am until 12 pm to work on these tasks. It was communicated to the team that during that time he was unavailable and unless the building was on fire, he wasn't to be disturbed. Then at 12 pm he'd take a break, have some lunch and only then get started with the rest of his to-do list, meetings and other priorities. Lucas also committed to not checking Slack, email or messages until after his lunch break. That's because there is never anything good there, it's all problems and other people wanting your attention. That in itself would risk mentally putting him in a reactive state, where he'd worry about other issues instead of focusing on his fundraising tasks. By sticking to this structure, he was able to defend his time, prioritize his high-value work and secure another multiple seven-figure raise.

I highly advise approaching your days and weeks in the same way. Going back to Section 1, think about your zone of genius, your current targets and what tasks you should be prioritizing. Think about how much time you need for this each week. What periods of the day are you the most focused, energized, and able to do your best work? This will give you a better idea of how you need to structure your days to allocate time for the big-picture tasks that need to get done.

The hardest part of staying consistent with this is going to be boundaries, not just with other people, but with yourself. After all, it's easy to convince yourself that something else is more important when you're caught up in the moment. Sure, there will be situations and circumstances where that is the case, and that's okay. But it's essential that deprioritizing your most high-value tasks is only done as an exception, not as a norm. Therefore, it's vital that you stick to a plan that minimizes distractions during your flow state.

So, think about what is likely to distract you or pull you off course. What could disrupt your focus? With that in mind, what boundaries and changes do you need to put in place? This will give you a better understanding of what you need to do to defend this time and ensure it is treated as the most important part of your day.

Energy-based scheduling

When it comes to planning, most people structure their days by scheduling tasks in their calendar gaps, mostly in order of priority or perceived importance. What they don't stop to think about is what their energy is likely to be or how they are likely to feel at that time. George was doing this constantly. In his attempt to rush through his planning, he'd just schedule tasks wherever he saw he had time. A prime example of where this backfired was on a day he knew he was going to have an intense board meeting. After it, he saw he had a couple of hours available, so he set aside that time to go through some detailed financial reports. By the time he got to them, he was mentally exhausted and simply didn't have the bandwidth to focus on this highly detailed task. I'm sure you've been there yourself, where you're mentally tapped out. So, something that should take 30 minutes takes two hours as you're not in the right frame of mind to get it done.

You can avoid these traps by being more intentional and proactive with what you schedule based on your bandwidth levels. That means before scheduling certain tasks, think about your energy and if you'll be able to execute those priorities at your best during that time. If you know you won't, then you need to allocate a different time for them elsewhere or change your diary so that you can ensure you have the energy to follow through. In hindsight, George's reports would've been best scheduled first thing the next day, as he'd be more focused and less likely to make errors. Getting this right will make a huge difference in what you get done, how much time you save and your ability to sustain your energy throughout the week.

Traffic Light Energy Tracker

In the next section, I'll share with you the tracker I use with my private clients to monitor their performance and figure out what we need to focus on to help them feel more in control. One tool you'll find in the performance tracker is the *Traffic Light Energy Tracker.*

Essentially, this is a traffic light system where the client reflects on their energy that day and assigns a color depending on their state of flow. When it comes to doing this yourself, you can make this judgment as follows: Green means everything ran smoothly, you were energized and moved through the day getting things done. Yellow is stop and start, not amazing, but not awful. Red is for days you struggle to get going. You're tired, unmotivated, have difficulty focusing and don't get much done.

I mentioned to you before that burnout comes from extended periods of pushing too hard, where the effects can compound and hit you like a bus. Often people can be feeling low on energy for weeks or months, but they're so busy they overlook the signs or don't recognize what is happening. From an energy management standpoint, you can keep on top of this by tracking your energy and monitoring how you are doing over the course of a week, month and longer.

That's why this simple strategy is so powerful, as it allows you to hone in on problems before they become bigger, long-term issues. For instance, let's say you have a few days straight with a mix of yellow and red days. Recognizing that makes it easier to stop and think about your current situation. Are you neglecting sleep? Have you been extra stressed? Is there an area of your life you are neglecting? From there, you can actively make changes to improve your routines, decisions and behaviors. Seeing a combination of reds and yellows could also be used as a sign and a trigger to take a break, have some time off or take a *pull* day to recharge. If you weren't tracking this though, you'd be completely unaware that there may be a problem. Instead, you'd just be going through the weeks, oblivious to the extent of how you have been feeling and risking continuing this pattern for weeks or months.

How you track this is up to you. You can do so in the daily reflection tracker that comes as a bonus with this book, drop color-coded pins into your calendar or any other way you want to approach this. The important thing is just being able to have a visual representation of how you've been doing over an extended period of time. Then, when you see fluctuations or drops in energy, commit to taking the time to figure out what is causing them. The benefit of doing this is that it forces you to think about your actions and whether you need to slow down or make some changes in how you're approaching your days.

Habits and routines

The strategies explained so far in this section will go a long way in helping you feel more in control. Long-term though, the biggest influencer on your longevity is going to be your habits, routines and the actions you take every single day. That's why one of the best things you can do is have an honest reflection of your life, where you look at what's out of alignment or where you're not being as consistent as you want (or need) to be with certain aspects of your life.

When I start working with a CEO, the first thing I help them do is gain clarity on the life they want to create. The way I approach it is to get them to think 90 days ahead and figure out the changes they want to make in their life and business. The reason I like to work with 90 days is because it's close enough in the future to be tangible, yet long enough to have a real impact and make progress. By thinking about who is the person that is living the life they want, we can then reverse engineer the journey This allows us to uncover the habits, behaviors and routines they developed to turn their vision into a reality. We can also then compare that to their current situation and think about what they need to stop doing or change, as it's holding them back from this bigger goal.

I highly advise taking some time to do this yourself. Think about your goals and the life you want to be living. Then ask yourself, what did the person you want to become do to make that happen? How are they spending their days? What are they doing with their time? Make sure you think holistically about all areas of your life. You'll no doubt get insights into everything from how to start your day to boundaries you need to set, ways to structure your time, find balance and prioritize what matters most.

Then look at your current situation. What is negatively impacting your energy? What is causing stress? What are you tolerating that is being a mental and emotional drain? These are going to be the areas you need to actively work on changing. Doing so will make it far easier to sustain your energy so that you can put it into the areas of your life that need it most.

Upon doing this, Liam had some huge realizations. He saw that to show up as the leader he wanted to be, he needed a strong start to the day. That meant getting up early, taking time to plan, defending his mornings and being intentional with his time. The thing getting in the way was him staying up late, causing him to oversleep and then rush into the day. What I reminded him was that his morning routine starts with the actions he takes the night before. That meant he needed a clear cut-off time to stop working, along with prioritizing ways to unwind and ensuring he was in bed by 10 pm to get enough sleep. Once we got that new routine in place, Liam was able to get up on time, plan his days and use the first two hours to focus on his high-value work.

This is why figuring out both the life you want and the version of you that made it happen is so important. From there, you can uncover the habits and routines you need to develop to turn it into a reality.

Task before moving forward

Take some time to think about:
1) What habits and routines do you need to develop to feel more in control of your life and business?
2) How does your energy fluctuate throughout the week and how could you implement *push* and *pull* days to avoid burning out?
3) What are your top priorities and high-value work? How much time do you need for these each week? When do you need to allocate time for these?
4) What else is draining your energy that you need to be intentional with getting under control?

Once you know this, then we can look at ways to effectively plan and structure your days to maximize what you get done.

Section 4

Effective Planning

The next area we need to focus on is how you plan your time. There's no way around it, if you want to maximize your days then effective planning will make or break your success. Despite that, you'd be amazed how many CEOs I speak to who, beyond having a to-do list, don't take the time to properly plan what they need to get done. This is a huge issue, because if you aren't intentional with what you take on, that's when you get involved in tasks you shouldn't, work on what you *feel* like doing, or tackle what seems important in the moment. This becomes even more of an issue the busier you get, as that's when planning tends to go out the window.

Remember Gary from earlier? The CEO who was presented with an opportunity to expand in another US state? One of the other challenges we tackled early in working together was his internal resistance to planning his days. He knew it was important, but with so much to do, he felt uncomfortable slowing down, as he saw that as time that could have been spent getting things done. Gary had built and scaled a business from nothing to doing close to 9 figures a year in revenue. Because of that, he was used to the hustle and grind it took to get it off the ground. If anything, it's where he felt comfortable. It's what he was used to doing.

This way of operating was also the very thing getting in the way of him taking the business to the next level. The reason being is Gary was highly reactive, which caused him to spend his days working *in* the business being the *doer*, instead of the *operator*. As a result, he had a very narrow view of what was going on, causing him to overlook huge issues that had developed in the team, their delivery and processes. That's the problem with being stuck in the trenches, as it's hard to plan your next attack when you can't even see the battlefield. In other words, your strategic decisions are hard to act upon when you're bogged down putting out fires. This is why for challenges, problems and opportunities to become clear, you have to slow down, step back and give yourself the time and space to fully process what is going on.

This is really what starts to separate founders and managers from CEOs, as if you want to be an effective CEO, then you have to become more intentional with spending your time in a way that serves your vision. This is hard to do when you're spending your days stretched thin, overwhelmed and in a constant rush to get things done.

For Gary this is where the accountability part of our work became so important, because if he was left to his own devices, he'd continue the cycle of just diving into his day. He made a commitment that he'd plan each morning. The agreement was that once he was done, he'd send me a quick message saying "planning completed". If I didn't hear from him by a certain time, then I'd send him a reminder. I know it sounds silly, but even CEOs need someone to hold them accountable for what they need to do.

Within a couple of weeks, Gary completely changed his perspective on planning. Instead of seeing it as a chore, he recognized that actually, this was his job. After all, the clarity he gained steered the direction of the entire business. By slowing down and planning he also started to see how many tasks he was involved in that he should've delegated long ago. In turn, this allowed him to remove himself and give his team more responsibilities, and therefore more opportunities to learn and excel. It also became clear that it was completely unnecessary for him to be working 60-hour weeks. In fact, once he got more intentional with what he needed to do, he nearly cut that in half, averaging around 35 hours.

This is why planning as a CEO can become your superpower, as the clarity you gain will directly determine the actions you take and the results you can create. It's also how you can ensure your priorities are in alignment and that you are fully utilizing your time to be effective with what you get done.

I know that planning is not the most glamorous of tasks. But I also know how important and impactful it can be. That's why I want to encourage you to make your planning time non-negotiable. To do this effectively, there are going to be three levels of planning that I'm going to take you through: monthly, weekly and daily. These will give you a complete overview of what is happening on a macro and a micro level, and if done correctly, they will massively impact your growth and success.

For you to be able to plan effectively, it's essential that you know your goals, priorities and what you are trying to achieve. After all, if you want to ensure you're moving in the right direction, then you need a target to aim at. To get this in place, I encourage my clients to set aside a morning at least once every 90 days to plan out their big, strategic goals. This is how they gain clarity on what their vision looks like for the next three months, and they can then use that to guide their actions, decisions and commitments.

Getting clear on your next 90 days

A CEO who found this process to be a game-changer was Alex. When we met, even though their business was growing month after month, he felt like he was spinning his wheels. Similar to Gary, he had no real agenda for what he took on and instead, he'd react or work on what was important in the moment. To make matters worse, his open-plan office was hectic, with warehouse staff constantly coming in to ask questions or to liaise with the sales team. This made it hard to fully focus or get in the zone. Because of all this, I suggested that he rent a meeting room in a coworking office so that he can plan their next 90 days. He agreed and communicated to the team that he'd be out for the morning, telling them that if they needed anything to either go to one of the managers, or to come see him in the afternoon when he returned. This allowed him to turn off his phone so that he could disconnect and concentrate.

That morning, he mapped out their next 90 days. In doing so, he uncovered new market opportunities, areas they were lagging and processes they needed to be more efficient. He also worked out their next hires, ways to reorganize the team and changes that could be implemented to help the business grow. He told me after that he couldn't believe the level of insight and clarity he gained from that one action. Since then, he's committed to doing this every quarter, as he's seen how essential it is to recalibrate and plan what is needed to deliver on the 90-day vision.

I'm a big advocate of changing your environment to do this, as sometimes you need a shift in energy to feel at ease so that you can think, be creative and be inspired. I've seen clients have success using anything from a rented meeting room to going to a coffee shop, using a hotel bar (it's usually quiet during the day) or even a client who goes to his lake house. That doesn't mean you can't do it from your usual office. Just be aware that sometimes it's hard to mentally shift into another gear when you're in an environment that is usually focused on firefighting and dealing with never-ending demands - basically, plenty of distractions. Either way, think about when and where you could map this out, then schedule time to make it happen.

How you approach this session is going to be different for every business. Think about your goals, vision and targets. What's working? What isn't? What challenges do you need to overcome? What are you not doing or acting on? What new campaigns do you need to implement? Where do you need support? What would need to happen in the next 90 days for it to be a success? This is going to give you a good idea about where to begin.

Generally, I recommend doing this at least once every 90 days. I have however had clients who realize this is one of their most important tasks, so they revisit their targets and strategy once a month. Ultimately, it's going to depend on you and your business, so test it and see what works for you. Once you know the priorities, that's when you can start planning and putting them into action.

Bonuses and resources

If you're anything like me and you prefer learning through visual aids or if you just want to dive into this deeper, I have a training video going through the *Effective CEO Planning Process.* It's yours as a free bonus for buying this book.

Throughout this section, I'll also be sharing screenshots from my *Effective CEO Digital Planner 2.0.* I'm using these as a guide to help illustrate and explain the concepts. I like this planner is because it keeps everything in one place. Also, you can keep it open in the background, making it easy to refer to whenever you need it. However, don't feel like you have to use it if it's not your style, as you can apply these concepts to whatever approach works for you.

You can access the training and download the planner at: **https://byronmorrison.com/ceobonuses**

The Effective CEO Planning Process

Monthly planning

Most CEOs I speak to know they should be planning their days and weeks (even if they've not succeeded in doing that before we start working together). Very few take this a step further and plan their months. While I don't mean planning every day of it, what I have found to be highly effective is having a rolling overview of the next 30 days so that you know the key deadlines, commitments and upcoming events in every area of your life.

When I got Jack to map this out, he saw that in two weeks he had a weekend trip away with his dad and son to attend a sporting event in another state. When looking ahead, he saw that two days after the trip he had a board meeting. Now, Jack was notorious for leaving his board reports and prep until the last minute. With how much time those tasks normally took him, he realized that, based on past behavior, he'd inevitably have to work a lot of that weekend. Meaning instead of being present with his dad and son, he'd be on his laptop or be mentally checked out worrying about how the report still wasn't done. To avoid that, he scheduled time the week before and set a deadline to get it finalized two days before the trip. By doing so he was able to go away and enjoy himself, all while avoiding the anxiety and stress that would have happened if he didn't plan accordingly.

This is why it's so important to be able to look ahead and know what is coming up. Because if you don't, you risk overlaps in commitments or deadlines creeping up that you then need to cram in or overextend yourself to get done. By having the foresight about what's on the horizon though, it becomes easier to make the right decisions, structure your time and balance key priorities.

In my *Effective CEO Planner 2.0*, you'll see a tab for monthly planning.

The Effective CEO: Monthly Planner

Date	Day	Event	Notes
01 May 2024	Wednesday		
02 May 2024	Thursday		
03 May 2024	Friday		
04 May 2024	Saturday		
05 May 2024	Sunday		
06 May 2024	Monday		
07 May 2024	Tuesday		
08 May 2024	Wednesday		
09 May 2024	Thursday		
10 May 2024	Friday		

The way to approach this is to look at all your commitments, deadlines and events for the next 30 days and add them in. This could include anything from a project deadline to your partner's birthday, a business trip or anything else that you need to be aware of or that will be a disruption to your usual routine. Then, in the notes, you can add anything you need to remember, do or prepare.

Getting this done shouldn't take long and the most time-consuming part is going to be the first time you do it. Since this is meant to be updated weekly, once Week 1 has passed, you can delete the last seven days, drag the dates down to add a new week and update it from there with any new events that you need to have in your 30-day rolling overview. You can also use this time to take a few moments to remind yourself what your next month looks like. This is going to allow you to know on a macro level what is incoming. You can then use this overview whenever you are presented with new opportunities or ideas, to see whether or not the timeframes align, or if they fit around your other commitments. This insight will make it far easier to make changes and shift things around if you decide to take on a new project.

Someone who avoided a tonne of headaches by doing this was Laura. On one of our calls, she told me about an event she was invited to attend and speak at in a couple of weeks. She was so excited about it since doing talks was something that she was passionate about and energized her, so we knew we needed to get this in her calendar. Her rolling schedule was already in place by this point, and when we looked at her diary, it clashed with their next product launch. Her company did these launches once a month and they were always full on, needing a lot of long hours and headspace. Laura was integral to them, meaning this wasn't something she could delegate. The launches also required a lot of moving parts from the team, including increasing advertising spend and running various campaigns to ensure they hit their revenue targets. With everything that went into them, it would be tough to make changes last minute, but since she saw the clash two weeks in advance, this gave them enough time to delay the launch by a week. This helped Laura avoid having to try and do multiple things while she was away at the event, and she could ensure she had the headspace and energy to make both successful.

I find that for most people having a rolling 30 days is more than enough. In some extreme cases, it may be worth looking further ahead. Patrick had taken over as CEO of a global corporation and part of his role required that at least a couple of times a year he visited their various locations. He found himself going through a crazy couple of months. One week he was in Australia, then two weeks later he had a trip to Europe. Three weeks after that he needed to go to New

Zealand. The commute and time zone shifts from the States were exhausting and he said "Never again". This is why for him we implemented a 90-day rolling calendar. By doing so, when planning these trips, he could look ahead to make sure they were always at least six weeks apart, giving him sufficient time to recover from jet lag and get back into his routine.

Weekly planning

To make weekly planning easier and more streamlined, you first need to add in your regularly occurring events and commitments. To do this, scroll down on the planner where you'll find a blank schedule (you could also use a blank calendar).

Average week							
Time	Monday	Tuesday	Wednesday	Thursday	Friday	Saturday	Sunday
06:00							
06:30							
07:00							
07:30							
08:00							
08:30							
09:00							
09:30							
10:00							
10:30							
11:00							
11:30							
12:00							
12:30							
13:00							
13:30							
14:00							
14:30							
15:00							
15:30							
16:00							
16:30							
17:00							
17:30							
18:00							
18:30							
19:00							
19:30							
20:00							
20:30							
21:00							
21:30							
22:00							

The next few subsections will help you fill this in and map out an average week.

Ideal Life Creation

If you're anything like the clients I work with, then a big driving force in your life is probably your desire to have freedom. But with so much on your plate, it can feel like something always has to give, and it's usually the things that matter most. I'm sure you've been there where you wake up filled with good intentions. Today you'll hit the gym, take the night off or finally get around to that hobby. Then things get away from you and today turns into tomorrow, then the next day, then the next. Now, it's inevitable this will happen from time to time, as there will be situations where something is more important. In a lot of cases though, it's happening frequently due to a lack of intentionality, boundaries and prioritization.

This is why when it comes to finding balance, I see most people approach it the wrong way, hoping they'll get it right. The reality is that *hope* is not a strategy and hoping you'll get time for your family, health and happiness risks them becoming the first things to get dropped. I've found that instead of trying to focus on *work-life balance*, we need to create *work-life harmony*. That's where I had the idea of what I call *Ideal Life Creation,* where you figure out the most important commitments and regular events in your life, and you schedule those first. Then you build everything else around that.

Getting this in place will depend on your company setup. Some people may have the flexibility to set their own hours, whereas others may be confined to a set work schedule like 9 to 5. Block off where you can't be flexible and then you can start adding all your *Ideal Life Creation* priorities. This could be anything from date night to gym sessions, playing golf, time with your kids, or anything else you want to do regularly.

Here's where the real magic happens. By having this structure mapped out, you can then become more intentional with what you schedule around it, making it easier to stick to. For instance, when Shaun came to me for help, he was having huge issues in his marriage. The crazy hours that came with scaling a company meant he hadn't been as present as he wanted or needed to be at home. He kept scheduling date nights to start reconnecting with his wife, but often he'd have to cancel to work late. To make matters worse, when date nights did happen, he'd be attached to his phone or thinking about work, which understandably caused further arguments and frustrations. When I looked at how his days were structured, I saw a pattern. Before date night he tended to have a string of meetings. These would either overrun, which was the cause of him having to cancel, or they'd be intense, so he'd then take that stressed energy with him to dinner. To turn this around, one of the changes we made was that on the days he scheduled date night, we restructured his diary to ensure that in the hours prior to dinner, instead of having meetings, he only took on less bandwidth and lower-stress tasks. This allowed him to make it home on time and he was also able to be more present, as he wasn't mentally on edge.

This is why what you schedule before these events is so important, because if you put the wrong tasks or commitments in, then you are going to set yourself up to fail. It's also important to recognize that with the responsibilities that come with your role, there will always be something in the moment that seems more important. That's why if you want to follow through with your *ideal life commitments*, then you have to raise your standards and make them a priority. Treat them the same way you would a meeting with your most important customer, where unless the building is on fire, you're going to make them happen. Remember, getting this right is all about proper planning, setting clear intentions and structuring your days in a way that makes it easier to follow through.

I find it can also help to do this with the other people in your life. For the last year, Nicholas and his wife were doing their best to balance his company with her career and an eight-month-old baby. With so much on, a lot of the things they wanted to do for themselves had slipped. What I uncovered was they were so busy rushing around, that they hadn't taken the time to slow down and communicate to the other person what help they needed, where they felt overloaded or what was important to them. He printed two copies of this calendar and they both mapped out their schedules, as well as the things they wanted to do for themselves. For him, it was time to work out and play piano. For her, it was to attend some weekly fitness classes and new-mother get-togethers. By knowing that, they were then able to align their priorities and ensure that the other was available during those times. Getting this in sync was the very thing they needed to get a resemblance of control back in their lives.

While having an average week mapped out is great, depending on your situation you may need to approach this with more foresight. Charlotte was sharing custody of her son, which meant she needed to be available to drop him off every other Monday and pick him up every other Friday. Because of that, she mapped out an average of 14 days in advance. That meant she could set expectations with her team about when she would be unavailable. This also made it easier to plan her weeks and other commitments as she knew these times couldn't be adjusted. Before doing this, on those days she'd generally rush around, be late or not get around to the tasks she was trying to cram in. She now manages to avoid all that by simply being more intentional and aware of what she takes on.

When you're planning your *Ideal Life Week,* it also helps to think about your routines. Remember the energy management section with strategies like *push* and *pull* days. This is the perfect time to schedule them, as it will be helpful to have them in place when it comes to planning everything else. Chances are you won't get this perfect straight away, and that's okay. Go with what feels right, as you can then test it and make adjustments accordingly. You may also need to adapt this during different seasons in your life and business. For instance, if you have an intense launch or project that requires additional time or disruption to your usual routine. In these times I find that it helps to sit down and map out a structure for this period. That way you can have a better understanding of how to approach it, rather than just pushing through and hoping for the best.

Adding work commitments

The next thing to add is the work commitments you have every week. I told you before about Lucas who needed to spend 9 am until 12 pm each day working on fundraising. While mapping out his average week, we blocked this off in his calendar so that he could defend that time. Think about your zone of genius and high-value work, how much time you need for them and when they need to get done. Scheduling these items first will make it far easier to prioritize them as the most important part of your week. This is how you can ensure that instead of just working *in* the business, you are working *on* it.

From there, add your regular meetings and events. When doing this you may see some overlap and clashes. I find that for a lot of CEOs, it's because they have allowed themselves to be too flexible and catered their schedule around others. As you've seen so far, if you want to be highly effective, then you must be defensive of your time. That's why this is a good opportunity to reschedule anything that doesn't align with how you need to be spending your days.

When I spoke to Sally about this, she realized she had various 1-2-1s scattered throughout the week. She'd scheduled them wherever she had time, without much thought about how that impacted her focus, energy and other priorities. With her new structure, she determined that she needed the first 90 minutes of the day defended for her zone of genius high-value work. Because of that, she had to move these around. In the end, she decided to schedule all of her 1-2-1s for a Monday. That way she could ensure the team had everything they needed for the week, and it freed her up to prioritize her other responsibilities. In hindsight, this was the clear solution, but it only became apparent when she slowed down and figured out how she needed to structure her time.

Look at what setup you need, along with what clashes or disrupts what you must do. It may not always be possible to change, as in some cases you may have meetings with investors or numerous stakeholders that can't be moved. Wherever you can though, build this schedule around what will work for you.

Getting this in place should, for the most part, be a once-and-done task. There may be times you need to go back and amend it, such as when priorities shift, or new responsibilities come your way. But this will give you a good idea about what an uninterrupted average week should look like before you add anything else.

On a side note, you may also want to look at this and see if there are any blocks of time you want to defend from having certain types of tasks scheduled in them. For instance, I have one CEO client who now doesn't take meetings until after 2 pm, so his schedule reflects that accordingly.

To help see in action, here's an example schedule of what a routine that includes all of the above could look like:

Time	Monday	Tuesday	Wednesday	Thursday	Friday
06:00	Wake Up		Pull morning		
06:30					
07:00	Work Out	Work Out		Work Out	Work Out
07:30					
08:00					
08:30					
09:00	Weekly Planning	HV Work		HV Work	HV Work
09:30					
10:00	HV work				
10:30					
11:00					
11:30					
12:00					
12:30					
13:00	SLT Meeting				
13:30					
14:00	1-1 Meeting				
14:30					
15:00	1-1 Meeting		Personal Time		
15:30					
16:00	1-1 Meeting				
16:30					
17:00	Wrap Up	Wrap Up		Wrap Up	Wrap Up
17:30					
18:00					
18:30					
19:00			Date Night		
19:30					
20:00					
20:30					
21:00					

Planning your weeks

When planning your weeks, the first thing you need to do is reassess your month's targets and key deadlines to remind yourself of your top priorities. This is key, as it will allow you to monitor your progress to ensure nothing is being overlooked. For instance, maybe you're on week three of the month and you realize you're behind on revenue. That may be a sign that you need to double down on generating new clients or sales activities to hit your targets. You can then prioritize these tasks in your planning and push back on anything that isn't essential right now.

The next thing to do is create a to-do list of what you need to get done. Then before you start to plan, take a few minutes to audit the list using the process from Section 1. Go through it point by point and ask yourself:

1) Is this actually important? As in will getting it done have a positive ROI, drive growth or impact the business? If no, remove it.
2) Is this a priority right now? Does it align with your 90-day goals and targets and do you have the energy and bandwidth to commit to this? If no, remove it from your list and set it aside for a later date.
3) If yes, does it need to be done by you?
4) If no, who could or should take over?

This will allow you to see what you need to delegate and let go of. It also helps to look at your upcoming week to uncover anything that is not a good use of your time or that doesn't get you closer to your targets.

When it comes to figuring out what to prioritize, one of my favorite questions to ask is: "Fast forward to 5 pm Friday, what would need to have happened for this week to be a success?" That can help you reverse engineer the week to know exactly what you need to achieve. From there you can fill out these boxes in the weekly planning tab.

Targets are any goal you want to hit that generally has a numerical outcome. Such as "x" amount of revenue, "x" number of new clients, etc. *Top priority* are tasks or projects that need to get done this week, such as board packs or looking at financial reports. *Radar* is anything you need to keep top of mind, but it isn't essential right now. *Study* is anything you want to learn this week. *To be completed* is anything you need to finalize. You may also want to add in life commitments as a reminder, like sorting your car insurance.

Having this mapped out will allow you to have a top-level view of what needs to happen this week. Then, looking at your diary commitments and average week, you can allocate these tasks to different days.

Monday	Tuesday	Wednesday	Thursday	Friday	Weekend
To do	To do	To do	To do	To do	To do
Other	Other	Other	Other	Other	Other

Generally, I find that if someone has more than two to three items to do in a day then it simply isn't going to happen. Especially between meetings, fires and other commitments. This is why it's so important to be realistic about what you take on.

Weekly (or daily) tasks

Henry was his own worst enemy with weekly planning. Every week he'd massively overestimate what he could complete. As a result, he'd overload himself and come the end of the week, he'd never even get close to finishing what he wanted. This just made him feel like he was failing, and he'd fall into a cycle of beating himself up, even though there was no way he could have done more. A lot of the pressure he was placing on himself was self-imposed, as he was the one setting the deadlines and crazy expectations. This is why I had to get him to be more realistic with what he took on.

To do that, I got him to look at how much available time he had that week. Let's say beyond meetings and other commitments, he had ten hours free. Then, for the remaining goals and other tasks that had yet to be added into the planner, I got him to think about how much time he needed to complete them. He needed to be realistic here, as often he'd underestimate how long something will take. Knowing that, he could then see that if he had 30 hours of tasks, but only ten available hours, then it was never going to happen. Meaning he'd either need to delegate more, free up space or accept that certain projects will take longer to deliver on. Recognizing this allowed him to take a huge amount of pressure off, relieving a lot of the anxiety that came with feeling like he wasn't doing enough. In addition, it helped him communicate and align better with his team on any deadlines and expectations where he would otherwise be a blocker. This relieved a lot of their frustrations, as previously failing to deliver on Henry's overly optimistic workload would then negatively impact their progress and priorities.

When allocating your time, it's also important to factor in tasks that you need to be consistent with each day to hit your targets, or because they're aligned with your vision. When Graham and I started working together he was running a $200 million revenue-a-year company. His big goal was that he wanted to sell and exit in the next three to five years. To make that happen, his focus needed to be on driving revenue and making the business as attractive as possible for potential buyers. Graham's zone of genius was business development, and the majority of their contracts came from the relationships he built. When we met though, he was so pulled into the day-to-day, that he barely had the time to nurture old relationships, let alone build new ones. Our focus was to get everything he shouldn't be doing off his plate so that he could spend the bulk of his time making calls, taking meetings and going to events. After a few weeks of action, we then had enough data to determine that each day he needed to call three new people and follow up with several previous conversations in order to ensure they hit their targets. These insights then meant he could schedule his day around these core actions.

Alongside scaling his start-up, Brad was trying to build a personal brand on LinkedIn. He saw this as a key activity, as being the face of the company helped open doors and brought new opportunities with investors. However, with so many other priorities and a lack of intentionality, he wasn't being consistent with making this happen. We figured out his daily actions, including writing and posting content, connecting with new people and responding to messages, along with how much time he needed to dedicate to these every day. This time was then blocked in his calendar on a daily basis, and the tasks were turned into a checklist. This approach made it easier to ensure everything was done, instead of it being something Brad *should* do, but never quite got around to.

The regular tasks you need to get done won't always be daily. For Victoria, one way she was growing her company was by attending events and going to lunches to build new relationships. While she had done great in the first part, what I uncovered was that she was dropping the ball when it came to following up. The simple solution was to schedule an hour for this every Tuesday and she blocked it in her calendar as a repeating task.

Not every day will be productive (and that's okay)

When looking at your week, there may also be a need to accept that not every day will move things forward. After all, with so many competing responsibilities as a CEO, there will be times when other commitments will take priority.

This is why I advise clients to view days as either *effective* or *efficient*. *Effective* days are where you focus on high-value work. You further your vision, drive growth and move forward what you need to do. *Efficient* days may be more operational. You attend meetings, do 1-2-1s, knock things off the to-do list and complete tasks that keep the business in order.

I find that often CEOs who are overwhelmed are stuck in a cycle where too many days are *efficient* and merely just getting stuff done, without enough prioritization on being *effective*. This happens when they get stuck focusing on what's important in the short-term or that day, without factoring in the vision and what they're trying to achieve at a macro level. I'm sure you know what it's like when you've got big-picture tasks that get put aside for something that seems more important in the moment. If you want to take your business to the next level or avoid losing your sanity, then you need a balance of *efficient and effective* days. This is why I advised you to take some time at the start of the week to reassess your goals, targets and priorities, along with what else you need to do. Taking time to be clear on this is how you can ensure that everything is in alignment.

By making a distinction between *effective* and *efficient* it also becomes easier to come to terms with what you are taking on. It also allows you to judge your progress over the course of a week, instead of a day. The way Arthur's company was set up meant most of his Monday was spent in back-to-back meetings. He barely had any free time, yet still, he'd cram more tasks into his planning, only to be left feeling like he was not doing enough. I pointed out to him that he was setting himself up for failure by viewing his priorities list as something that needed to be completed in one day. By changing his perspective to view Mondays as *efficient* days, it became easier to accept the limitations of what he could do. Even more so when he recognized that this day freed him up to have *effective* days the rest of the week.

Andy was spending most of his time on Tuesdays and Thursdays in various meetings with his team, stakeholders and customers. Despite how busy he was, like Arthur, he'd still try to take on more, then he'd beat himself up that he wasn't being productive enough. By making a distinction between the days, he was able to have so much more control over how he structured his week, grouping tasks with a similar purpose on days intended for solving them. Also, knowing Tuesdays and Thursdays would be intense, he could implement measures to ensure that he was more prepared. That meant taking time the day before to think through each meeting and planning for them in advance.

When to plan

When it comes to weekly planning there's no right time to do this. Instead, you need to figure out what works for you. I find that for most clients this is generally on a Sunday as they're able to slow down and think through what they want to get done that week. Some clients though prefer to do it as their first task on a Monday to set them up for the week ahead. I've even had some who do it Friday as it allows them to go into the weekend feeling relaxed knowing they have a game plan in place to hit the ground running on Monday. It really doesn't matter when you do it, as long as it's done. So, think about when you're most likely to be consistent with it, then commit to that. I find that the weekly planning itself generally takes around 30 minutes. Just remember to start by updating your rolling month, revisiting your priorities and looking ahead to see if there is anything you need to factor in for those next seven days.

With a lot of clients, I've found that many choose to get their assistant involved, as they then know their priorities, what they have coming up and where they need support. For instance, if you have a big deadline on Thursday, then your assistant will know to defend your diary and not allow other meetings to creep in. Or maybe they see some other tasks that they could take off your plate.

Whether you do this yourself or with your PA, I have some prompts to help you think about the week ahead:

1) What do I need to get done by 5 pm Friday for this week to be a success?
2) Because of that my biggest focus this week is...
3) What challenges do I see coming up this week?
4) How will I address them?
5) What actions do I need to take this week to show up as my best self?
6) What do I need to remind myself about my goals, self and journey?
7) Additional help and support I may need this week is...

The reason I've included these prompts is because they actively force you to stop and think about what you are signing up for. They can also highlight areas where you need to be more prepared, conversations you need to have, or actions you need to take. Let's say next week you have a big launch. You know it's going to be long hours and very stressful. By looking ahead, you can determine that you need to be strict with your diet and sleep schedule to ensure you feel your best. You also need extra support in arranging your meals or handling other tasks, which your assistant can help pick up. Recognizing this in advance means that you can arrange this now, rather than just reacting and trying to do it all yourself.

Daily Planning

The final step is planning your day. The reason you need to revisit your plan daily is to set your intentions for the day ahead. You can also look at your schedule and see if anything changed, or if your priorities shifted from earlier in the week.

When using the digital planner, I find that most people tend to just use the weekly planning tab, as everything is in one place and it's easy to work from. I know everyone is different though, which is why you'll also find a daily planning tab. If you are going to use this section, I advise starting by filling out the time blocks with your average day commitments, and other meetings and tasks (you can copy and paste this from the weekly tab). Then, by looking at what available time you have and your priorities, you can plan accordingly.

How to do the planning

Regardless of how productive or efficient you are, there is always going to be *more* that needs to be done. This can very easily keep you in a headspace where you feel like no matter what you do, it's never enough. That's why just like in the weekly planning, one of my favorite questions to ask each day is: "Fast forward to 6 pm, what would I need to get done for this day to be a success?" Just like before, by thinking ahead you can reverse engineer your key priorities. Then come the end of the day, it makes it easier to feel at peace, as you know you moved forward what you intended. During this time, you can also think about what you need in place to set yourself up for the day ahead.

Maybe you have some meetings you need to prepare for, or a tough conversation you need to think about how to handle.

One of my clients, Jeffrey, is terrible when it comes to sticking to daily planning. He generally works late, so he oversleeps or takes a while to fully wake up. This often causes him to have a slow start to the morning, making him feel like he has to rush to start his day. He knows he's way more effective when he slows down and plans, yet still, he often lets it slide. Jeffrey also told me that until he has his first meeting of the day it's hard to get focused and in the zone. To help ensure my clients have everything they need, I'll sometimes do a couple of calls with their assistants to look at how they support them and to figure out ways to optimize and improve the process. I did this for Jeffrey and by knowing how he operates, I suggested to his assistant that she schedule a daily morning meeting where together they go through his day. This was highly effective, as not only did it force him to plan, it also allowed her to know his priorities and how to support him. Best of all, it also triggered the first meeting he needed to get focused on the day ahead.

I also had to coach Jeffrey's assistant through the reality that CEOs need accountability. I explained to her that as CEO, Jeffrey had no one holding him to the things he needed to do. This is why he could let priorities slip or drop what he was doing for something that seemed more important in the moment. Because of that, I told her that the most valuable thing she could do for him was to *manage* him. That meant pushing back when he overcommits. Holding him to his core responsibilities. Asking him the right questions to get him to think. This was a huge breakthrough and confidence builder for her, as prior to our conversation she didn't want to overstep or interfere with what he was doing, when actually, it was exactly what he needed.

To help her make the best use of their morning meetings, I gave her some prompts to get clear on what the day looked like and their priorities. You can use these yourself every morning to ensure you've set yourself up for success.

1) Fast forward to the end of the day, what would need to happen for it to be a success?
2) What are today's top goals/priorities?
3) What challenges, situations or stress do you see yourself facing?
4) What do you need to prepare to handle them?
5) What help and support do you need?

By spending 15 minutes going through his tasks, upcoming meetings and other commitments, Jeffrey was able to break the cycle of just diving into the day and allowing life to happen to him. In turn, this allowed him to get more of the *right* stuff done, all while feeling more in control.

I highly advise making this morning planning something you do before you start your day. Yes, I know you're busy, but if you think about the bigger picture in an eight plus hour day, do you really not have 10 to 15 minutes to figure out how you are going to spend that time? It's like an elite athlete. They don't just step up to the plate, take a shot and hope for the best. Instead, they slow down, focus, play it out in their head and create a plan of attack. If you want to perform at your best, then you have to treat how you approach your day in the same way. After all, the insights you gain will directly determine what you take on and get done.

One thing I also advise is to sense check how you feel when you finish your planning. If what you have in place feels manageable then great, you're good to go. If you feel overwhelmed or anxious, then it's a sign you've overloaded yourself and that you are taking on far too much. Realizing that, you can take a moment to figure out what else could be delegated, what tasks aren't essential, or where you need to push back. Acknowledging this at the start of the day can have a huge impact on your stress, headspace and emotional state.

When it comes to daily planning, you don't necessarily need to do it in the morning either. I've seen some CEOs make this one of their final tasks to round off their day. By doing so, they can go away knowing what they need to do tomorrow. If you choose to approach it this way, just make sure you take a few minutes in the morning to revisit the plan. During this time, check that nothing has changed and also remind yourself what lies ahead.

On a final note, I know that there will be days where despite the perfect plan or your best intentions, something will come up, causing the day to get away from you. It's part of life and an inevitable aspect of your role. When this happens, what matters most is how you respond and what you do to bounce back. Noah runs a highly reactive business where staff are constantly asking for his support and insights to handle clients' cases. In a perfect world, he'd get to the office and plan his day before 9 am, but sometimes people would ask for his help as soon as he got in the door. I found that on the days he got disrupted, he'd then feel rushed and convince himself that he was too behind and that there was no point in doing his planning. This would cause him to be all over the place, diving into issues he shouldn't or that weren't aligned with his key priorities. That's why we determined that this planning needed to be the first thing he did when he sat at his desk, even if he got derailed and only got there at 12 pm.

There will also be times when fires and issues come up that throw your plans out the window. This is why daily planning is so essential. Let's say yesterday something came up that needed your immediate attention, so you didn't get to your other tasks. By sitting down today you can then reallocate that time and shift priorities accordingly. This is how you can still move things forward, even in imperfect or volatile conditions.

Daily reflection

When you're running a company it's easy to get stuck in a cycle where you're so busy, that you're just trying to get through the day, without giving any thought to how it went or what you've accomplished. The situations, circumstances and events you went through though are your greatest opportunities for growth. Often, it's through them that you uncover mistakes you made and find ways to improve for the future.

This is why when I'm working with CEOs, daily reflection is a core component of how I approach helping them become more effective in their role. In the *Effective CEO Planner 2.0,* you'll find the daily reflection tracker I use to monitor everything from how my clients managed their time to ways they handled tough conversations and what threw them off their game. Then in our weekly calls, we take time to discuss these challenges, looking at what they need to learn and how to navigate similar situations in the future.

The way I always describe this approach to clients is it's a lot like an elite athlete going back to watch old game footage. By revisiting what happened, that's how they can figure out ways to improve and get an edge. If you want to perform at the highest level, then you need to approach it the same way. In the reflection planner, you'll find a series of questions. These are the ones I initially use with clients. They are:

1) What went well? / What situations or tasks did I handle well?
2) What did I realize or learn?
3) What could I have done better?
4) What would have allowed me to feel more in control?
5) What do I need to do or be intentional about tomorrow?

Depending on someone's challenges and situation, I may change, add or remove certain questions. For instance, if someone is struggling with boundaries, then I may include something like: "Were any boundaries overstepped today? If so, what do I need to do about it?" This forces them to look back on what happened, the context of that event, and we can see where these boundaries need to be enforced going forward. Another common one is: "Were there any tough conversations I should have had that I avoided? If so, why?"

Benjamin often found himself being unfocused, so when doing this with him I added: "What disrupted my time today?". This question helped us uncover that one of his biggest disruptors was the newly hired finance director whom he was supporting in settling into the role. The trouble was that he was constantly interrupting him with questions, and even coming into his office whenever he had a query. As a result, Benjamin would be pulled out of his flow state and more often than not he'd find it difficult to get back into it. To solve this problem he set a boundary with his finance director, telling him to make a note of any questions and they scheduled time to sit down once a day to go through them.

For Joshua, we uncovered that the biggest disruptor to his productivity was the anxiety that came with having tough conversations. On the days he knew he needed to address an issue, he'd often fixate on the problem and worry about it to the point he wouldn't get anything else done. Knowing that, we put a plan in place where in the morning, he'd prepare for the conversation, figuring out exactly what he needed to say. Doing so put him at ease, making it easier to then go about his day. Wherever possible he also reorganized his day to deal with these discussions as early as possible so that there was minimal anxiety for the rest of his day.

From these examples, you can see that if these leaders hadn't reflected on how they spent their time, then they never would have picked up on these patterns. Meaning they would have just allowed them to continue impacting their focus, productivity and performance. When I'm working with clients I'm generally the one who recognizes correlations, lag indicators or problems we need to monitor. To do this yourself, you need to think about what is currently impacting your performance. For instance, if you know you struggle with defending your time, setting boundaries or facing tough conversations, then these will be challenges you want to take time to process and reflect on. Figuring this out will help you determine what questions you need to add.

In the tracker, you'll find two drop-down options for energy and productivity to rate them on a scale of 1-10. You'll also see a *flow* column with a color menu of green, yellow and red. This is based on the traffic light system I took you through in the energy management section. By monitoring this you can then look at your energy and performance over the course of a week (or longer) to watch for signs that you may be pushing too hard or approaching burnout. This makes it easier to catch problems before they become severe, and you can also figure out why they are happening. For instance, if your energy and productivity are down, you may recognize you haven't been prioritizing proper sleep or meals. Picking up on this now can then help you get back on track with habits and routines you let slip.

The reason I advise filling this out daily is because it's easy to forget what happened today, let alone a week ago, and therefore *why* you may have felt or behaved one way or another. This risks overlooking key issues you need to process and learn from. The task itself shouldn't take more than five minutes. Then, at the end of each week, go back through it and look for correlations, repeating patterns or anything that is flagging an issue you need to be aware of. You can then use those insights to become more intentional about what you need to do or work on going forward.

I've found that with private clients this activity is where their biggest growth happens. It helps to uncover challenges, lag indicators and problems they would otherwise have overlooked. By revisiting and discussing them, we can then figure out how they can improve, which in turn, builds their intuition and makes them more confident in navigating similar challenges in the future.

Coaching these leaders through the challenges we have identified is also my superpower. From thousands of hours coaching and working with clients in 17 countries, I've been part of conversations that very few people in the world are aware of, let alone have been exposed to. This gives me a unique experience, perspective and insight that I'm able to use to help clients navigate challenges and deal with problems in a way they can't get from anywhere else. In order to do that effectively, I've found that I need to be able to monitor and uncover what is truly going on with their mindset, performance and day-to-day. That's why I love this tracker and it's one of the tools I use to do exactly that during our calls.

There's no way around it. If you want to become more effective in your role then you have to take time to reflect and process what you did. That's why I highly encourage you to set aside time each day to do this task, as the insights you gain could be the most powerful tool in your growth.

Tasks before moving forward

Decide where, when and how you need to approach planning your months, weeks and days. As I mentioned at the start, one option is to use the *Effective CEO Digital Planner 2.0*. If that doesn't work for you, then you can apply these concepts to whatever approach you want to use. Just make sure you schedule these actions and commit to doing them consistently.

If you want to revisit how to plan on a deeper level, then you can check out the *CEO Planning Process Training* that comes as a free bonus with this book.

You can access that, as well as download the digital planner at:
https://byronmorrison.com/ceobonuses

Section 5

Becoming More Effective

You now have all the strategies you need to figure out how to spend your time, properly delegate, manage your workload and plan your days. You should be good to go now, right? Not quite. Have you ever thought about why you can give 100 people the same strategy, yet they all get different results? If the strategy is the same, then what's the difference? It's the mindset of the person implementing the strategy, as the way you think, process problems and make decisions is what will ultimately determine your ability to execute and follow through.

That's why the next step in this journey is to focus on removing (or reducing) all the things that are going to get in the way of you becoming a more effective CEO. I've taken some of the biggest reoccurring challenges and disruptors that I see derailing CEOs' days and I'm going to break them down one at a time. This section is going to be more of a quick-fire round, moving through how to deal with different problems and scenarios. Before we get to any of that though, we first need to address the mindset behind defending your time.

Defending your time

If you're anything like the CEOs I work with, then you probably want to be the leader people can turn to for guidance and support. While this is admirable, it brings with it huge consequences. Even more so when you're constantly dropping what you need to do to solve other people's problems or to help everyone else but yourself. This is why one of the biggest challenges you will face when it comes to defending your time is being at peace with doing so. Because I get it, you feel guilty and like you don't want to let other people down. The reality is though that often your actions can do the opposite, especially since your team, stakeholders and customers are counting on you to run and grow your company. Their future, livelihoods and success depend on it. Because of that, prioritizing the things *you* need to do is not selfish. If anything, it's selfish not to.

I've had to talk so many CEOs around to this way of thinking, which is why I know that it's something you'll likely have to come to terms with as well. If you don't, you'll continue going into the day with a plan for what you need to do, then not follow through. Or you'll spend most of your time putting out fires or being pulled into issues that aren't driving growth.

That's what was happening to Peter. He'd start his mornings filled with good intentions about how he was going to spend his time. Then people would keep walking into his office and coming to him with problems. He wanted to be a nice guy who supported others, so he'd constantly stop what he was doing to fix whatever they needed help with. After years of behaving this way, his people-pleasing tendencies were tearing him up inside. He'd now started to resent the constant interruptions, as he knew he'd either have to work late, or not make progress on his other tasks. This resentment just made him feel worse about himself, further amplifying the guilt over the thought of letting people down.

A lot of the work we had to do together revolved around boundaries. The first big shift was starting to handle issues on *his agenda*, not other people's. That meant that if someone came in his office with a problem, rather than immediately diving in to help, he'd tell them to come back at a time he was available to talk. When he was working on high-focus tasks, he'd close his door and get his secretary to take messages and ensure he wasn't disturbed. He'd also put his phone on airplane mode so that he wasn't interrupted by calls when he was trying to do something else.

Initially, it was very uncomfortable for him to do. What he found was that very few of those issues needed immediate attention. If anything, he recognized that he was the only one making matters feel urgent, by jumping on the task straight away. In reality, this was just another job his team needed to complete *at some point* that day or that week. Recognizing that the company didn't fall apart by him not diving straight in took a huge amount of pressure off of him. Even more so when prioritizing his own work led to further growth.

On one of our calls, Jacob told me how frustrated he was with a meeting he had at 9 am that morning. His HR manager reached out saying she needed to speak to him urgently, so he canceled his focus time to meet with her. It turned out, all she wanted was to discuss some time off and to approve her holiday. This completely threw off his morning routine when he was at his most productive, all for something that really wasn't a priority. Sure, it may have been important to her, but it could have waited until later that day. This for Jacob was the wake-up call that he had to make himself less available. He set a new boundary that he didn't take internal meetings until after a certain time. He also asked for context whenever someone asked to meet with him so that he could gauge how important something was. This made it far easier to know when to push back. It also helped him determine when issues needed immediate attention, making it easier to justify when to derail his initial plans.

The reality is that if you want *to be a more effective CEO, then you have to get comfortable with saying no and pushing back.* This will become even more important as you scale, especially since a growing team risks even more people vying for your attention. Every CEO's approach is different, so getting this right will depend on your situation. Let's go through how other leaders started defending their time.

Theo kept having people walking in his office or emailing asking to speak to him. A boundary we put in place was that rather than dealing with them immediately, he'd look at his schedule and tell people what time he could help. A way that worked amazingly for Nathan was every morning he messaged the team on Slack saying when he had availability. These were the open-door hours that people could come in with any questions or for issues they needed support on. This simple 20-second action saved him hours each week as he stopped being disrupted. Elizabeth had grown a company from just her to a team of over 40. She'd been the one to get most of their customers, many of whom had been with them for years. Because of that, they were used to dealing with her, so they'd message or call her directly instead of going through the service team. This meant she'd get bombarded with calls and messages, all of which were a distraction from what she needed to get done. The solution was to set an autoresponder on WhatsApp and a voicemail giving them the number for who they needed to contact instead. This was a simple way of communicating the new process to customers and it stopped her from having to live on her phone or deal with problems that should be picked up by a member of her team.

The thing with setting boundaries is that it's easy to convince yourself that they're a bigger deal than they are. In most cases, people respect them and will adhere to them. The reason why they aren't doing that right now is often because you haven't communicated that there is an issue to begin with or set a new expectation about what needs to happen. At the end of the day, saying no or helping others on your agenda doesn't make you a bad person or a bad leader. If anything, it's part of you stepping into your role and owning the position you have taken on.

Getting this right is going to be one of the biggest factors in you becoming more effective with your time. Because of that, take some time to think about: What are the biggest disruptors to your focus and productivity? Where do you need to become better at defending your time? What boundaries do you need to set?

Figuring this out is going to give you a better understanding of the changes you need to make. It'll also help you identify how your days get disrupted and what to do better to defend your time.

Daily wrap up

With so much on his plate, Ryan constantly found himself in a cycle where he'd have to work during the evening to catch up on everyday tasks. This included everything from responding to messages and emails, admin work and other responsibilities that he struggled to get around to during the day. Because the day got away from him, he'd then spend most of dinner mentally checked out thinking about what he still needed to get done. Then he'd sacrifice time with his family as he'd have to go get on top of everything. Understandably, this was having a huge impact on his home life. All of these tasks had to be done, but because of how his days were structured, he kept hoping he'd be able to cram them in or that he'd find time for them during working hours. This rarely happened, which is why it was clear we had to carve out that time and treat it as a priority. What I got him to do was block out the final hour of each day and schedule it as *wrap-up time* (for him that was 4-5 pm). During this time, he'd be unavailable for any meetings. That time was meant for catching up on emails and messages, reflecting on the day and planning for tomorrow. This allowed him to then go into the evening feeling relaxed as he had everything handled.

To implement this you need to:
1) Figure out the daily tasks you need to keep on top of.
2) Be realistic with how long you need for them (generally it's 30 to 60 minutes).
3) Block off the time in your calendar.

For this to actually work, you have to be highly defensive with this time. Especially since when you're busy, chances are you'll convince yourself that something else is more important in the moment. Sure, in some cases that will be true. But if it keeps happening daily then it's a big red flag that you need to get better at defending your time and not overloading yourself.

To make it more likely you'll follow through, I also advise setting a reminder to pre-empt this time. That could be a notification 15 to 30 minutes beforehand focused on: "What do I need to finish up or do so that I can start wrapping up?" This will allow you to have an easier time transitioning to this part of your day.

Running effective meetings

One of the biggest frustrations I hear from CEOs is how much of their time is spent in endless meetings that don't achieve anything. To make matters worse, they go on too long, draining their energy and bandwidth, which negatively impacts everything else they need to get done. If anything, meetings are probably the part of the role that you dislike the most. Because of that, so many people just attend them with the mentality of getting through them. Viewing and approaching meetings that way is not a good use of your time, energy or resources. If you look at the best CEOs though, when it comes to meetings, they're fully present and engaged. They ask great questions and ensure that everyone is focused on achieving a goal. You can't do any of that if you're unprepared, don't have a plan in place, or if you're getting distracted on your phone responding to emails. This is why if you want your meetings to be an effective use of time, then you have to become more intentional with how they're spent. This is why I always advise clients to take a more intentional approach to this part of their role. That includes having a clear focus, structure and boundaries on allocated time.

To do this yourself, it's firstly essential that you figure out in advance what the purpose and outcome of the meeting is. Take some time to consider the current challenges, what needs to be discussed and the key points which need to be addressed. This will enable you to create an agenda for what will be covered. Not only will this ensure that you can maximize the time, you can make it even more effective by sharing this with people in advance. That way they can prepare, bring with them any relevant information or determine any questions they need to ask.

Knowing the outcome you want is going to come through preparation. Whether it's before the meeting, earlier in the day or week, allocate time to understand what you are aiming to get out of the people in the room during your time together. I know it's not the most glamorous of tasks, but you need a clear focus, otherwise you risk wasting time or trying to figure it out as you go along. Being clear on the outcome also makes it easier to keep everyone's focus on track. That way, if people start drifting off topic you can pull them back on course. Also, if a new idea is introduced or a different challenge comes up, then you can always table it or arrange another time to discuss it rather than diverting the focus.

Secondly, you need to set time expectations. The reality is that if you give someone an hour, they will find a way to talk for an hour. If you give them 30 minutes, they will be more honed in and on point. Because of that, tell people up front how much time is available. I've found that shorter meeting times also make people more likely to address the issue at hand. Whereas if they perceive there's no rush, that's when they tend to waste time making small talk, catching up about their weekend or discussing the weather. There's a time and place for building rapport and in a meeting isn't it. If people have a defined outcome and they know there's a limited time to find a solution, that's when it becomes easier to get them to operate with more intention and urgency.

Setting boundaries with time works with phone conversations as well. A CEO I worked with who ran a large company serving clients wanted to make sure he provided them with everything they needed. This meant he would often take calls where he'd allow them to drag on, making him late for everything else. The advice I gave him was to set boundaries with his time at the beginning of the call. Initially, he was worried this wouldn't go down well, but by starting calls saying how much time he had or when he had a hard stop, he actually found people were highly respectful. No one thought he was being rude when he'd have to finish the call or increase the pace of their conversation to solve problems in the available timeframe.

Thirdly, implement what I call the *25% rule*. Most meetings tend to be run without a real structure. Because of that, time gets away from people and meetings are either rushed at the end, or worse, they don't have a clear resolution. I'm sure you've been there where a meeting goes from 1 to 2 pm. Then a couple of minutes before the end, people panic that time is nearly up and they scramble to finish, often allowing it to overrun. This is where the *25% rule* comes in. When you have 25% of the meeting left, start transitioning towards wrapping up. So, if the meeting is an hour, after 45 minutes communicate that "We have 15 minutes left, what else do we need to cover?" Figure out the next steps, answer questions, set deadlines and ensure that everyone has what they need to move forward. By doing so you'll ensure those last few minutes are laser-focused and outcome-driven, instead of rushing to cram everything in.

One pattern I see with CEOs I work with is that they will often have blocks of back-to-back meetings. The problem with this approach is that it can leave them bouncing around from one thing to the next, barely having a moment to think, let alone deload or prepare for the next meeting. This structure also means that if anything overruns, they're then spending the rest of their day feeling like they're behind. In a perfect world, we'd solve this by adding buffers to give you a gap to slow down and recalibrate before moving on to the next thing. However, if you have six meetings in a row, then a 10-minute buffer is going to add an hour to your day, which let's be honest, is time you don't have. Given how time-poor CEOs are, I've found that a better approach to *adding* buffers to your schedule is to *make* them. You do that by reducing your meeting times, so rather than a 60-minute meeting, you reduce them to 50 or 55 minutes. Rather than 30, 25. The key part to getting this right is sticking to your hard stop. You do that by using the *25% rule* to ensure people have what they need at the end so that you can then move on and close the meeting.

Resetting your intention between tasks

Part of the problem with rushing around to get things done, is it's easy for you to become highly reactive, diving into tasks without much thought about their context or how much priority you should give them. This can cause you to make mistakes, focus on problems you shouldn't or overlook key aspects of what you need to get done. This is why from a high-performance standpoint, I advise taking time to reset your intention between tasks by taking a moment to refocus.

The way to do this is after every big task, meeting or commitment, take a few minutes to slow down. Start by taking 60 to 90 seconds to just stop and breathe. The reason conscious breathing is so important is because when you're operating at pace, your blood pressure increases and your cortisol goes up. This can make it harder to think clearly or make the right decisions. By taking time to take deep breaths in and out, you can lower these levels, allowing you to feel more grounded and at ease.

Then take a moment to think about what you need to do next. Whether it's a meeting, working on a report or anything else you need to tackle. Think about what is the outcome you want. What do you need to get done? What challenges may come up? This will enable you to mentally prepare for what is next. It's like an athlete stepping up to take a shot. They don't just hit the ball. Instead, they take a few swings, playing it out in their mind and preparing themselves for what they are about to do. For instance, let's say you need to look at a report. Think about what is the purpose of going through it. What information are you looking for? What could disrupt you? Thinking about this before diving in will give you a better idea of how to set yourself up for approaching the task in a way that allows you to complete it effectively. It'll also help you remove distractions, as it will be a reminder to close your email and turn off your phone so that you can focus. Or if you're going into another meeting, even if you prepared for it earlier, take a moment to remind yourself of the outcome. What do you need to communicate? What questions do you need to ask? What do you need to clarify? Regardless of what you are about to jump into, take 30 to 60 seconds to think about it before you begin.

I call the combination of this breathing and refocusing *The Intention Reset Technique*. This process will allow you to recalibrate, clear your mind and get clear on your next task. Doing this won't take more than 3-4 minutes and it'll allow you to become far more intentional with what you take on.

Recalibration periods

In the planning section, I shared with you that one of my favorite ways to approach the day is to reverse-engineer it. In the morning ask yourself "What do I need to get done by 6 pm for today to be a success?" While it's great to set the focus upfront, the reality is that things can change, or new challenges can come up. This is why it helps to reassess and recalibrate to ensure your focus is in the right place. After lunch or at a set time, reflect on your progress. Think about what you've crossed off your to-do list already, what is outstanding and what you need to prioritize next. This will allow you to refocus and ensure you are putting your energy into what actually matters. Also, if you've got a commitment like a dinner reservation or attending an event, then this is a great time to ask yourself "What do I still need to get done to leave by 5 pm?" This will make it easier to ensure that you're on track and that you can finish on time.

Taking periods throughout the day to recalibrate and reset your intention is going to help you feel far more focused and in control. Even though this is hugely impactful, I know from experience that habits like this are the hardest to stick to, especially when you feel like you have no time. This is why you need to be highly intentional with making them happen. The easiest way? Schedule them. Add a reminder in your calendar, a notification on your phone, or even a sticky note telling you to stop and breathe. Whatever you need to keep these actions top of mind.

Getting people to solve their own problems

Andrew was running a global production company and one of his biggest challenges was people coming into his office with issues. It was never-ending, and often he was being bombarded with problems that he shouldn't have even been involved in. Like when someone came to ask him what to do about a broken car window. What was even more frustrating for Andrew was that in many cases, he wasn't even the best person to ask about a lot of these issues. For instance, if someone had a logistics problem, he was barely involved in that department. That meant he'd then have to waste more time speaking to others to try to understand the process before he could even look at a resolution.

It wasn't just lower-level employees dumping problems on his desk, it was his managers as well. Part of the issue was that Andrew was allowing this to happen. I explained to him that he'd essentially created a culture where people didn't have to think for themselves. Why would they take time to figure it out when they know they could just pass it on to him? To combat that, he had to start pushing back. What he implemented was a new rule. You could only bring him problems if you also came with a potential solution as well. He found that this policy dramatically reduced the amount of people coming to his office. This was because it forced people to take ownership of resolving their own issues, often meaning they found solutions without needing his support. In the situations they did come to him for help, it also reframed the conversation from him having to figure out a solution, to discussing viable options and determining the way forward.

One of my favorite strategies to use when someone comes to you with a problem is to tell them to research it, think of three potential solutions and then come back with their recommendations. Then, if needed, you can discuss it with them and determine which of their suggestions is the best path of action. The reason this is so effective is it forces people to look at a variety of ways they can solve a problem. By doing so, much like Andrew, you'll find that people will often figure it out on their own without needing further support from you. This is also why defending your time and solving problems on your agenda is so essential.

I've had so many CEOs realize that by pushing back, people then find ways to fix their issues themselves. Meaning that just by saying "not now", you're giving your team the time and space to solve the problem on their own - and they often do. Something that wouldn't have happened if you dived right in to resolve random problems straight away.

A big part of effective leadership is empowering people to think for themselves, especially when they're meant to be the ones with expertise in a particular area. You are never going to get out of the weeds or stop working *in* the business though if you keep allowing yourself to be pulled into everything. This is why you have to set boundaries, be clear on expectations and ensure people are delivering on the jobs you are paying them to do. Of course, there will be exceptions, such as when an issue arises that has huge consequences or that only you can make a decision on. In those cases, you'll need to be the one who takes ownership of the situation. Just don't let that become the norm, especially when the problem at hand is small in the context of your role and your business.

Dealing with overwhelm

99.9% of the time when someone tells me they are OVERwhelmed, they're actually UNDERplanned. The reason being is they haven't slowed down to figure out what needs to happen to complete the outstanding tasks. To make matters worse, being underplanned also makes them fixate on the outcome or end result. This in itself is a huge trigger for anxiety, as instead of thinking about step one, it causes them to worry about step five and everything that needs to happen in between.

When I'm working with clients as part of my coaching program, I offer *SOS calls*. These are calls designed to deal with immediate problems that can't wait until our next session. The biggest use of these calls is to help CEOs work out how to navigate tough conversations. The second, is when they feel overwhelmed by a huge workload and they are unsure what to prioritize or where to begin.

A perfect example of this was an SOS call I had with David. One morning he messaged me at 11 am as he was struggling to focus. I had an opening in my diary at that time, so we were on a call a couple of minutes later. David started to tell me about everything he needed to get done that day, from preparing board reports to signing off on a campaign. He also needed to call the dentist and sort out his car insurance. All these competing priorities had caused him to mentally shut down, to the point he'd wasted the first two hours of the day just procrastinating.

What I got him to do was list off everything from the reports to the campaigns and the personal life admin. Once we had it written down, I then went through it point by point, asking him to detail to me the steps needed to complete each task. This forced him to slow down and think methodically about solving the items on his to-do list. The result of this was a game plan of what David needed to do step-by-step to make headway in his day. Not only that, it also eliminated the overwhelm, as it made his workload feel far more manageable. Doing all this only took 10 minutes, but it saved him hours that day that he likely would have lost to overthinking or being stuck in analysis paralysis.

When people are overwhelmed, they tend to convince themselves they can't slow down, when actually, that's the time they need to most. Overwhelm often causes decision paralysis, which then for some, also translates into anxiety and further spiraling feelings of a loss of control. During those times, my favourite strategy to deal with this is the simplest. Get a pen and paper and do a brain dump of everything going on in your head. Make sure you include all your life and business tasks that are causing you to feel on edge. The benefit of doing this is that by getting all these tasks down in front of you, you can consciously disconnect from them. So instead of battling scattered, racing thoughts and bouncing between them in your head, you can then address them one at a time. Go through each line asking yourself what needs to happen for this job to be crossed off? What's the outcome you want? What's the first thing that needs to get done? This will allow you to create a plan and gain clarity over your priorities.

This approach has saved clients countless headaches and it's a simple way you can get focused and feel more in control of your days. This is also one of my favorite strategies to use at the end of a day and week. By getting everything out of your head, it makes it easier to then walk away and disconnect for the evening or weekend. Especially since you know you have a plan to come back to. While it isn't a miracle cure, I've also seen clients who struggle with restless nights improve their sleep through this approach, since work-related worries would keep them up into the late hours of the night. So test it, as this can go a long way to putting you at ease.

Breaking through procrastination

One of the biggest risks to your success is procrastination. I'm sure you know what it's like when you know you need to do something, but you just can't bring yourself to do it. Whether it's working on that report, having that tough conversation or simply doing admin tasks, it can feel like having to climb a mountain just to get started. You'd be amazed how often I speak to CEOs who are losing hours every single day avoiding the things they know they should be doing. This isn't just costing them growth and revenue, it's also coming at the expense of time with their family and enjoying life. The worst part is that most of these tasks won't even take long to do. Or once you get started, you'll get in the zone and it'll be easy to carry on. Despite knowing that still, you struggle to get going.

Often the advice given to deal with procrastination is to remind yourself *why* you need to do something. "Think of your family, goals and vision, use that as your motivation!" The problem with this approach is that what you have to gain is not enough of a motivator to push through what you're procrastinating on. I'll use an easy-to-follow health example. Everyone knows you need to exercise and eat better to live a longer life. Yet one of the areas most people struggle with is eating the right foods and moving enough. A big part of the reason why is that subconsciously they view the discomfort of the actions they need to take as more painful than the benefits of what they have to gain.

This is why I'm not a big fan of using *feel-good* as a motivator. Instead, I'm a much bigger advocate of *amplifying the pain*. One example I always give to clients when explaining this concept is a day where I'd done everything that I needed to do, except work out. It had been a crazy day, with back-to-back meetings, intense client calls and various other fires. I was exhausted and I wanted nothing more than to sit on the couch and watch TV. I knew all the reasons why I *should* go to the gym - the endorphins, the stress relief, the muscle growth, overall better health. That didn't make me want to face it though. What I did instead was think ahead to the end of the day and how I would feel if I didn't go. Fitness is a big part of my life and knowing myself, at 9 pm I'd beat myself up that I didn't just get it done when I had the time for it. Knowing I didn't want to end my day feeling frustrated and annoyed with myself for failing to work out, I used that as the motivation to push myself to go to the gym.

Focusing on future pain works for everything that you don't want to get started on. Like that report you've got in your drafts. Think about how if you delay, then you'll have to work late instead of spending time with your partner or kids. Or that tough conversation you don't want to have. Think about the anxious and sleepless night you'll have playing it out in your head, worrying and making up scenarios that may never come true. You can break the procrastination cycle by putting yourself in future-you's shoes. Imagine the negative feelings they'll have to go through or how they will feel when they'll have to sacrifice or miss out on something important in order for you to avoid taking action right now.

Amplifying the pain works for deeper mental blocks as well. For instance, maybe a fear of failure or rejection is stopping you from picking up the phone to call potential clients or investors. Think about six months from now, when your inaction causes you to close down the business. How you can't provide for your family. How you let down your team and those around you. The reason this works is you're tipping the scale in the other direction, making it more painful *not* to take action. That's what then makes is easier to follow through on your task.

I shared this with a client recently who for the past two days, had been avoiding drafting a legal letter. He knew it wouldn't take long, but it was boring, tedious and something he didn't want to have to think about. I asked him what would happen if he continued delaying and he realized that he'd be thinking about it all night. That he wouldn't be present at dinner. That he wouldn't be able to switch off and sleep. That the next day he'd also then have to get lawyers involved and it would drag on. He texted me an hour after our session saying it was done, as he didn't want to feel or deal with any of that later in the day. When he was just thinking about what he didn't want to do, it was easy to just avoid it. When he shifted to what would happen as a result of not taking action, then it became easier to just get it done.

Beyond avoiding future pain, I've also got another strategy I love to use. I spoke to you earlier in this book about how every new level of success is going to require a new level of you. This is why when I'm working with clients, the first thing we figure out is who they need to become to create the life, business and success they want. We can then use that clarity to reverse engineer the journey, figuring out the exact habits, routines, mindset and way of operating they need to become the next-level version of themselves.

The next step in this is getting them to take action and make decisions based on what that version of them would do, instead of who they currently are. In practice, what that means is when they're faced with something they don't want to do, they have to ask themselves "What would the CEO I want to become do right now?" Then they have to push themselves to take that action, since the *Evolved CEO* version wouldn't sit on something like this.

This works because is it takes what *you* want and how *you* feel out of the equation. Rather than relying on motivation, discipline or willpower, you act on your future reality. You act in the interest of someone else, your *future you*. For instance, let's say you're in an intense meeting and you want to share something, but you are worried about doing so. In that moment you risk self-doubt preventing you from speaking up. Ask yourself "What would the leader I want to become do right now?" Will they stay quiet, or ask the question that will clarify this specific point for everyone else in the room? Or if you don't want to go for that run or hit the gym, ask yourself "What would the person who has the body I want do in that moment?" Would they have made excuses and put off their workout, or would they just do it, even if they didn't feel like it? Or let's say you're at an event and you want to go speak to that person or potential customer, but you're nervous and that lack of confidence is talking you out of going to introduce yourself. "What would the person who has the results I want do right now?

You can apply this to every area of your life, from facing that task, clearing your inbox, having that tough conversation or setting that boundary. I'm not saying it's easy, but when you start taking action as the person you want to be, that's how you become that person. It also empowers you to make choices based on the life and outcome you want, rather than your current situation, fears or reality.

Keeping yourself accountable

If you want to live a life that other people never will, you have to be willing to do the things that other people won't. That includes facing the boring everyday actions that you'd rather not be doing. Going back to the elite athlete's example, a big contributor to their success is that they are consistent, where every day, rain or shine, they uphold the standards of what they need to get done to keep pushing their boundaries. In many ways, building a business needs to be treated in the same way. After all, it is often the consistency of doing the not-so-glamorous tasks that will sustain momentum and lead to growth, no matter the weather or who is watching.

This is also where accountability can play a big factor in your success. A lot of clients find it easy to procrastinate when they don't have anyone holding them to what they need to do. This is why with my clients, we regularly agree to timeframes and deadlines for completing specific tasks. Then, I send reminders or chase them to ensure they get them done. I find that a lot of the time just knowing they need to check in or feedback is the very thing that pushes them to follow through. So, if you don't have anyone keeping you accountable, figure out who could play that role for you, or what that could look like and make it happen.

Final thoughts

All of these strategies are going to go a long way in helping you defend your time and to maximize what you can get done. But they will only work if you commit to following through with them. Because of that, take some time to reflect on your days and weeks to identify what is getting in the way of your goals. From there, start creating a plan of the changes you need to make to remove or reduce your blockers, regardless of what they are.

Section 6

Evolving As A CEO

You've probably heard the saying "What got you to where you are, isn't going to get you to where you want to be." This is especially true when you're a CEO, as what made you a great founder or manager, may make you ineffective in this role. This isn't just the case for new CEOs in startups, as it continues to be a risk as you scale. Changing dynamics, expectations and commitments require you to adapt how you approach new and often more challenging situations, to continue getting results and being the leader you want to be. This lack of adaptation is something I see repeatedly, where CEOs who don't properly transition into their new responsibilities inevitably bottleneck growth.

To make sure that doesn't happen to you, the final section of this book is going to talk you through what you need to do to evolve into the leader your business needs to take it to the next level of success. From working with CEOs in 17 countries, I've discovered that there are three areas you need to develop if you want to become an effective CEO and leader. These three areas are your mindset, emotional control and leadership/performance.

Another way to illustrate these is in the form of these three pillars:

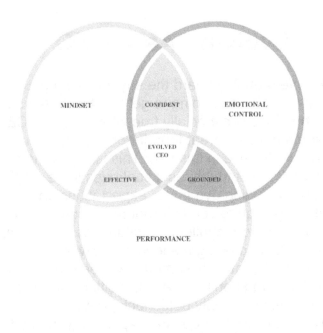

What I've found is that most overwhelmed CEOs tend to only work on one or sometimes two of these pillars. Ignoring any part of this three-way structure is problematic, because...

You can have the right mindset and be super productive, but if you can't control the stress or deal with the pressure, it's going to keep you trapped in a reactive state of fight or flight where you're controlled by your emotions.

Or you can be really organized and grounded, but if you don't believe in yourself, then you'll keep second-guessing what you're doing, avoiding making decisions and not taking the actions you know you need to take.

Or you can mentally and emotionally be in the right place, but if you don't know how to manage and defend your time, then you'll spend your days stretched thin and feeling like no matter what you do, you're always behind.

If your role currently feels out of your control and you're not performing at the level that you want, I'd be willing to bet you're missing one or more of these pillars.

I shared with you at the beginning of this book that one of my favorite quotes is "Your business growth will never outgrow your inner growth." The reality is you will continue feeling stressed, overwhelmed and in over your head until you level up the areas that are holding you back.

Another way to look at it is to think about your old laptop. Remember how when you got it, it worked great? It was fast and could handle everything you needed. After a while though, it started to slow down. Its memory wasn't as good as it used to be. It struggled handling multiple tasks at once and if you put too much pressure on it, it would crash and stop working altogether. This is exactly what's happening with you, as your mindset, emotional control and leadership skills are outdated and struggling to keep up with the new levels of challenges that come with your growth. It's why you're stuck in the weeds, overthinking and at times feeling like your business is a mental and emotional drain.

So how do you fix this? Like that old laptop, you need to upgrade, to evolve. You do that by focusing on all three of these pillars. By building a solid foundation in each of them you'll be able to maximize your time, lead with confidence and ultimately grow a business without losing your sanity.

This book has primarily been focused on the pillar of leadership and performance, with some aspects of mindset. If however, you want to reach your full potential, then you need to develop in all of the areas. To help CEOs do exactly that, over the last few years, I've developed a battle-tested five-step process called the *Evolved Method* that is built around these three pillars.

The Evolved Method

In this book, I've shared various case studies and client stories with you about CEOs I've helped to navigate the challenges that come with their growth. All of them have implemented my *Evolved Method* and it's how they've evolved into the leader their business needs to take it to the next level of success.

Because does this sound like the situation you're in right now?

- You're feeling stretched thin, overloaded and overwhelmed by everything that needs to get done
- You have so many competing priorities that you often get stuck spinning your wheels or doing tasks that don't lead to growth
- You're highly reactive and a lot of your days are spent putting out fires and dealing with other people's problems
- You get times where you overthink, second guess yourself, struggle making decisions and procrastinate over what you know you need to do
- You're not clearly communicating, setting expectations or keeping people accountable
- You struggle with balance and even when you do take time off you're attached to phone thinking about work
- You're feeling stretched thin, overloaded and overwhelmed by everything that needs to get done

- You have so many competing priorities that you often get stuck spinning your wheels or doing tasks that don't lead to growth
- You're highly reactive and a lot of your days are spent putting out fires and dealing with other people's problems
- You get times where you overthink, second guess yourself, struggle making decisions and procrastinate, avoiding what you know you need to do
- You're not clearly communicating, setting expectations or keeping people accountable
- You struggle with balance and even when you do take time off you're attached to phone thinking about work

If this sounds like you, then I'd love to take a moment to talk you through this process and how beyond this book, I can help you. Because if we were to work together, then this is what we'd go through to help you take control and become more effective in your role.

Step 1: Identity Upgrade

We all have a way in which we view ourselves, our beliefs about who we are and what we can and can't do. Often this identity is what keeps you consistent with the actions and behaviors that align with how you see yourself and the way you live your life. The problem with this is that what made you who you are today, isn't going to help you become who you're meant to be tomorrow. If anything, your current way of doing things may be the very reason why you're stuck or not performing at the level you could or need to.

This is why the first thing we need to do is figure out who you need to become to take your life and business to the next level. Who is that version of you who shows up powerfully, makes better decisions, leads with confidence and lives a life of freedom on their terms. Using that clarity, we can then reverse engineer the journey, figuring out the exact habits, behaviors, beliefs and non-negotiables you need to take on to evolve into that next-level version of yourself. This will enable us to create a game plan of exactly what you need to do (and stop doing) every single day to create the life, business, freedom and success that you want.

Step 2: Develop a CEO Mindset

When you're scaling a team and company it's easy for your days to become all about putting out fires, solving other people's issues and dealing with never-ending demands. As you've no doubt seen, there's no way you can make the right decisions, effectively lead or show up as your best in this reactive state.

There's a huge difference between a reaction and a response. A reaction is impulsive and driven by emotion. A response is processed and controlled.

This is why we need to focus on upgrading your way of thinking, to develop the CEO mindset that is grounded in a state of response. By doing so, when faced with challenges, instead of reacting, you can stop, process problems, understand the situation and only then choose how you respond to it. Not only will this put you more in control of your emotions, it'll also help you stay calm, confident and composed when navigating the challenges that are thrown your way.

Step 3: Rewire sabotaging thought patterns

The side effect of being under so much pressure to perform and deliver is that you can get stuck in your own head. It can be paralyzing, causing you to overthink, second guess yourself, feel like an imposter and procrastinate, avoiding what you need to do.

All of this is linked to your subconscious mind filling your head with mental barriers that are causing you to get in your own way and sabotage yourself. This is why you need to rewire your subconscious mind to replace the doubts and fears with new levels of confidence and self-belief. We also need to build your intuition, so that you can trust your gut and follow through with what you know you need to do.

Step 4: Amplify your performance

We need to figure out where you spend your time and what you should be focusing on and prioritizing. From there you can implement the right processes and systems to effectively delegate, manage your workload, structure your days and defend your time.

We'll also look at ensuring you can clearly communicate, set expectations, keep people accountable and install feedback loops to ensure they follow through. This is how we can get you out of the weeds, so you can stop working in the business and start driving growth. I'll also give you tools and techniques to help you stay focused, maintain energy, manage stress and everything else you need to consistently perform at your best.

Step 5: Ideal life creation

Let's be honest, running a business can take a huge amount out of you. Despite your best intentions, it can always feel like something has to give, and it's usually the things that matter most. To make matters worse, even when you do take time off, you're attached to your phone and thinking about work. Before long, this can leave you feeling like your business is a mental and emotional drain. After all, if you can't enjoy the success you worked so hard for, then what's the point?

That's why we are going to figure out what a life of freedom on your terms looks like and then build everything else around that. We'll focus on developing the right routines, setting boundaries and ensuring you can avoid burning out, find balance and have more joy in your life.

This process is how I'm going to help you evolve into the leader your business needs. By the end you'll change the way you think, how you process problems, communicate and navigate challenges. You'll be able to make better decisions, lead with confidence, set the right boundaries and trust your intuition. You'll be more focused, get more done, manage your workload and consistently perform at the level needed to be a highly effective CEO. As a result, you'll start showing up as the leader you need to be to create more growth, make more impact and have more freedom to enjoy the success you worked so hard for.

One question I'm often asked is "Have you worked with people in my industry?" While it's a valid question, I need to remind you that I'm not a business coach and I'm not going to come in and tell you how to run your company. Instead, I'm going to put the focus on you and how you show up in everything you do. Because of that, the industry you are in is actually irrelevant, as managing people, navigating tough conversations and everything else we need to focus on is going to be the same. This in itself though is why I've been able to work with such a variety of clients. The Evolved Method has been implemented by everyone from tech CEOs to CEOs running global production companies, SAAS and AI companies, financial institutions, 7-figure agencies, real estate businesses and billion-dollar unicorns in Silicon Valley.

This allows me to bring a varied and unique perspective to help you deal with the challenges in front of you. This is key, because if you look at all the best leaders, CEOs and athletes in the world, the one thing they all have in common is that they surround themselves with the right support. They know they need people to challenge them, to get them to think differently and push them to reach their full potential. They also recognize that you need someone external to help uncover blind spots and figure out your lag indicators. Not only that, but at times you also need someone external who is detached from the situation to see it for what it truly is.

This is where my superpower comes in. Over the last decade, I've spent 1000s of hours working with clients on situations that very few people in the world will be aware of, let alone be exposed to. This has allowed me to develop a unique experience and expertise that I'll be able to use to help you navigate challenges unique to you.

With that in mind, based on what you've learned in this book and seeing how I help clients, do you think that if you spent the next 90 days with me you'd become more effective in your role? Do you think it would have a positive impact on your life and business?

If you answered yes, then we should talk. The best thing to do is set up a time to speak directly to me.

You can through my website at:
https://www.byronmorrison.com/evolved-program

You can also get in touch at
byron@byronmorrison.com

When you schedule a time we'll hop on Zoom, have a friendly conversation about your situation and from there we can see if working together is the right fit. If not, I'll be able to point you in the right direction.

Now you may be thinking "Byron this sounds great, but I'm so busy I don't know if it's the right time or if I can take this on as well right now." I get it, and as you can imagine time is one of the biggest challenges for the clients I work with. That's why I want to assure you the work we do is not about adding more to your plate. Instead, it's about making you more effective in everything you do. I find that my average client gets back five to 15 hours a week. That's time they can then spend driving more growth, creating more revenue and living the life of freedom they want. So, if you don't think you have time to do it, then that's a sign that you don't have time *not* to.

Client success stories

Throughout this book, I've shared client stories and case studies where due to confidentiality reasons, I changed all of their names. On my website though you can find various video testimonials from CEOs who have gone through this process, and below I share a glimpse of what they had to say. With these, their real names are used and you can watch their full videos on my website:

Cole (CEO): *"When something so transformative or someone so transformative enters your life it's really hard to put that impact in words right and that's that's how I felt about this entire experience working with you...As a Founder as a CEO as a person I could not more highly recommend working with Byron because it'll change your life, it's as simple as that. It couldn't be more of an honor or a pleasure to be able to call him a coach, a mentor a friend and a person you won't meet many people if any people in your life who are better human beings than this man is. So thank you Byron for everything that you've done everything you continue to do."*

Ron (CEO): *"After working with Byron and him offering the tools and rewiring my mindset, I have now come back as a more confident leader, I have learned how to defend my schedule, I've learned how to be less reactive, but to also to be able to just pause and look at situations and come up with a better plan, a better solution. I've set new standards...and I'm very confident that Byron is going to change your life for the better".*

Jordan (CEO): *"When I first started working with Byron, I really didn't feel like I was where I wanted to be. I felt like things were out of control, I didn't know how to get my life of working 80 hours and was struggling to spend enough time with my family. I was really trying to get that back, and what I found was that so much of what I didn't feel in control of, I had the ability to get in control of by changing the way I thought about things, by changing the way I approached situations, how present I was, having a true vision for my future, having action plan that really allowed me to recapture that control, to get organised, to come into meetings and be with my family, everything improved."*

Max (Tech CEO): *"Honestly, it's been one of the best decisions I've made. Certainly, compared to the financial investment the value that's come out of it has been astounding."*

Tyler (Business owner): *"I feel like I've left this universe and gone into a different one. It's been incredible…If you judge my level of happiness, clarity, sleep cycle, relationships, confidence, or every other area of my life, it's an easy win. My direction in life has completely changed".*

Rosemary (Business leader): *"I don't feel like I have control back, I feel like I have it for the first time. I used to be fighting all these fires and battles and it was exhausting. As everything felt out of my control and I was miserable. Now I feel calm and like that fire is merely a distraction that I know I can handle."*

Michael (CEO): *"I've gone from completely tired, exhausted, drained to back to my old self so to speak and with more purpose. I'm glad I did it, I certainly know that if I didn't, I'd probably still be in that state of unhappiness and stress. It was the best money I've ever spent on myself".*

Neil (Business owner): *"I now feel completely different, I feel clear-headed and able to focus on the stuff I work out that I should be focusing on, I don't jump around anywhere near as much...I'm in control".*

Lauren (CEO): "You said you'd make me a better leader and you did. The time we've spent has been invaluable and our sessions are always exactly what I need to calibrate and process problems",

Josh (Business leader): "*People around me recognised that I'm more effective than I've ever been".*

To find out more on how I can help you go to:
https://www.byronmorrison.com/evolved-program

You can also get in touch at:
byron@byronmorrison.com

Closing thoughts

We've covered a lot in our time together and you now know exactly what you need to do to maximize your time, manage your workload and take control of your role.

I know that this is a lot to process, so if you haven't already, make sure you access the bonuses. You'll get everything from the CEO Planning Process Training to videos on how to audit your time and The Effective CEO Digital Planner and more.

Get them now at:

https://byronmorrison.com/ceobonuses

To help you further on this journey, I put out content on a variety of channels.

You can connect with me further on:

LinkedIn

https://www.linkedin.com/in/authorbyronmorrison/

Join my *Impact Driven CEOs* Facebook community at:

https://www.facebook.com/groups/impactdrivenceo s

I also have a series on YouTube focused on becoming a more effective CEO which you can watch at:

https://www.youtube.com/@ByronMorrison
Other books

CEO In Control is book two in this series. Master the mental game needed to be a highly effective CEO, as you discover how to stop reacting, get out of your own head and take control of your role.

Maybe You Should Give Up is about overcoming self-sabotage. You'll discover 7 ways to get out of your own way and take control of your life.

Final Words

Thank you again for getting this book and I hope you enjoyed reading it as much as I enjoyed writing it.

I know leaving reviews is a hassle, but they're also essential in enabling me to reach and help more people with my work. That's why if you wouldn't mind taking a moment to leave a review and rating on Amazon, I would beyond appreciate it.

I look forward to our paths crossing and if you have any questions about what I covered in this book or anything else, drop me an email at **byron@byronmorrison.com** and I'll personally respond.

Wishing you continued happiness and success,

Byron

Made in the USA
Monee, IL
17 December 2024